The
WAX MELT
Workbook

Zoe George

First Published in Great Britain in 2021
Copyright © 2021 Zoe George

The author has asserted their right under the Copyright, Designs and Patent Act 1988 to be identified as the author of this work. This book is a work of fiction and any resemblance to actual persons living or dead, is purely coincidental.

All rights reserved. No part of this publication may be reproduced or transmitted in any form or by any means, electronic or mechanical, including photocopy, recording, or any information storage and retrieval system, without permission in writing from the publisher.

A CIP catalogue record for this book is available from the British Library

ISBN 979-874529-029-9

Cover Design by Creative Covers
Typesetting by Book Polishers

Disclaimer

The author has provided their interpretation of the legislation referred to in this publication, and this interpretation does not constitute financial, legal or medical advice.

The author is not responsible for any liability, loss or risk, personal or otherwise which may arise, directly or indirectly, from reliance on information contained in this publication.

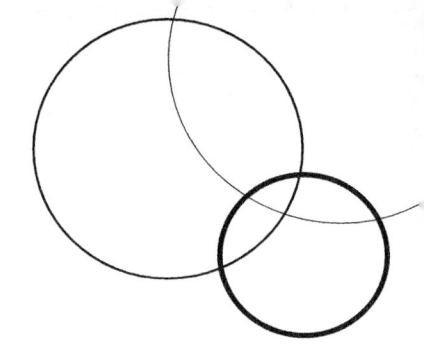

Contents

Author's note	**7**
Introduction	**9**
Part 1: Getting Started	**13**
1.1 What is a wax melt?	15
1.2 Why make wax melts?	15
1.3 Do you want to start selling?	16
1.4 Safety precautions	16
1.5 Safety Data Sheets	18
1.6 Disposing of unwanted materials	23
1.7 Disposing of used wax melts	23
Part 2: Materials and equipment	**25**
2.1 Waxes	28
2.2 Paraffin Waxes	29
2.3 Plant-based Waxes	30
2.4 Cure times	32
2.5 The 'natural' wax debate	32
2.6 Wax melt formats, moulds and containers	35
2.7 Silicone moulds	36
2.8 Plastic moulds	36
2.9 Container melts	37
2.10 Creative melt formats	37
2.11 Wax melt packaging	39
2.12 Labelling your wax melts	40
2.13 Fragrance oils	41

2.14 Calculating fragrance load	41
2.15 Fragrance families	42
2.16 Fragrance themes and collections	43
2.17 Essential oils	44
2.18 Colours and decorations	46
2.19 Dyes	46
2.20 Mica	47
2.21 Glitter	48
2.22 Other decorations	49
2.23 Equipment	51
2.24 Weighing	52
2.25 Melting	52
2.26 Pouring and stirring	53
2.27 Protection and cleaning up	53

Part 3: Projects — 55

PROJECT 1: Deli pot wax melts	59
PROJECT 2: Heart shaped wax melts	61
PROJECT 3: Marbling effects	62
PROJECT 4: Ombre effects	64
PROJECT 5: Wax brittle	65
PROJECT 6: Wax Crumble	67
PROJECT 7: Scoopable wax	69
PROJECT 8: Squeezable wax	71
PROJECT 9: Layered scoopable wax pie	72
PROJECT 10: Hanging wax tablets	74
PROJECT 11: Simmering granules	76
PROJECT 12 : Mini diffusers	77

Part 4: Legislation — 79

4.1 Legislation	81
4.2 CLP	82
4.3 How does CLP apply to wax melt makers?	83
4.4 How does CLP work practically?	83
4.5 Labelling elements	85

4.6 Can I use the same pictograms and statements on every label?	87
4.7 So which pictograms and statements do I use?	87
4.8 Are there any cases in which I do not need a CLP label?	88
4.9 Other labelling	89
4.10 Food Imitation Regulations 1989	90
4.11 Intellectual Property	92
4.12 Consumer Rights Act 2015	95
4.13 Consumer Contracts Regulations 2013	97
4.14 Trading Standards	98
4.15 Trading status	98
4.16 Insurance	99
4.17 The importance of record keeping	99
4.18 Invoices and receipts	100
4.19 Batch records	100
4.20 Suppliers batch numbers	100
4.21 Providing good customer service	101

Part 5: Build your brand — 105

5.1 Build your brand	107
5.2 Create a brand you love	107
5.3 Find your voice	108
5.4 Refine your brand	108
5.5 Other branding aspects to consider	110
5.6 Getting help from professionals	111
5.7 Establish your brand	111
5.8 Product packaging	111
5.9 Purchase extras	112
5.10 Social media	112
5.11 Online selling platforms	113
5.12 Your own website	114
5.13 Events and exhibitions	114
5.14 Maintaining your presence	115

5.15 Customer feedback	116
5.16 Keeping up with trends	116
5.17 Promotions	116
5.18 Wax-melt challenges	117
5.19 Wax-melt parties	117
5.20 Brand representatives	118
5.21 Collaborations	118
5.22 Donating to charities	119

Part 6: Expansion — 123

6.1 Expanding your range	125
6.2 Add-ons	125
6.3 Scented sachets	126
6.4 Wax tablets	126
6.5 Simmering granules	127
6.6 Room sprays	127
6.7 Diffusers	128
6.8 Burners	128
6.9 Bath and body products	128
6.10 Other products	130

Worksheets — 131

Worksheet 1: Supplies List	133
Worksheet 2: Wax Testing Record	134
Worksheet 3: Batch Record	135
Worksheet 4: Website Comparison	136
Worksheet 5: Brand Design	137
Worksheet 6: Pre-launch Checklist	138

Troubleshooting	**139**
Suppliers and resources	**145**
Interviews	**153**
Before you go…	**165**
Acknowledgments	**167**
About the author	**169**

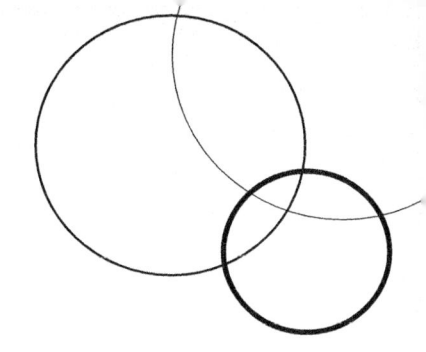

Author's note

At the time of writing, the International Fragrance Association (IFRA) had amended its Code of Practice regarding the criteria for the safe use of fragrance ingredients, which includes the use of fragrance oils to make home fragrance products. This particular amendment (also known as Amendment 49) affects the maximum fragrance loads for products that use fragrance oils, including candles, reed diffusers and wax melts. If you make and/or sell any of the home fragrance products mentioned in this book, please ensure you do so in accordance with the most up-to-date IFRA-recommended percentages; this information is usually found together with the supplier's SDS documentation. If you are not sure, ask the supplier to confirm.

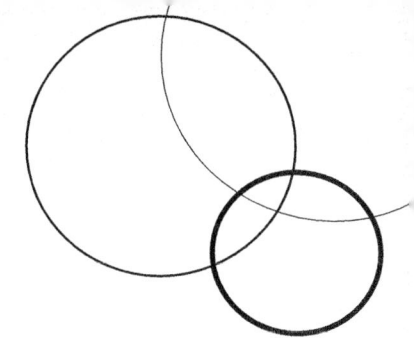

Introduction

So you want to make wax melts?

I am so happy you have chosen my book to help you!

Get ready to discover hundreds of fragrances, decorate with glitter in all colours of the rainbow and experiment with different wax textures like scoopable wax. Wax melt making is highly addictive and, once you get the balance right, can be a profitable pastime.

I wish a book like this existed when I first started to make wax melts several years ago. I had just created an Instagram account and 'liked' a few pictures of handmade candles. Instagram – being Instagram – began to populate my feed with more candle pictures and other little wax objects. I had to take a closer look: at the time I had no idea what wax melts were, let alone how to make them. They looked like flattened crayons to me. As a perfume addict, I was also interested in the vast range of scents that these wax melts came in. Melts that smell just like that high-end perfume? *Yes please* ... melts that smelled of freshly baked gingerbread? *Add to basket*!

One day I typed "how to make wax melts" into Google.

I had amassed quite a collection and being a crafter at heart I wanted to try making wax melts myself. You can guess what happened next. Within a month, boxes of various waxes were squeezed into my tiny London kitchen, plastic jugs and bottles of fragrance oils stacked upon shelves and random wax melts appeared out of nowhere.

I made up samples and wrote lots of illegible notes and six months later I had built up a following on Instagram and Facebook, selling my melts to customers all over the UK.

Several *years* later and here I am, typing away next to a newly delivered box of fragrance oils. There is a huge cardboard box in the shed, filled with silicone moulds of all shapes and sizes, a half-empty sack of packing peanuts perched on top.

I have gained a lot of experience in wax melt making and selling over the years, and want to share that knowledge with you, so I hope you find The Wax Melt Workbook a trusted and inspiring resource.

Using *The Wax Melt Workbook*

Feel free to write in The Wax Melt Workbook and highlight sections as you go along. This is a workbook after all, and you will get more from it if you record your progress. It is your book, for your journey!

Part 1 of the Workbook guides you through the initial stages and safety information.

Part 2 goes through the supplies you need to start making your first wax melts.

Part 3 contains twelve projects (from basic through to expert) to hone your skills.

Part 4 covers the legal considerations of selling wax melts in the UK.

Part 5 takes you through the steps needed to build your business and brand.

Part 6 looks at ways in which you can expand your range.

There are **Things to think about** at the end of sections to aid your understanding and **Worksheets** to record testing and other information.

Troubleshooting provides solutions to the most common problems encountered when making wax melts, and a list of **Suppliers** is also included as a good starting point for buying materials and equipment.

There are **Interviews** with two popular suppliers for you to also enjoy.

Join the online wax melt-making world

Online wax melt-making communities such as those found on Facebook can be an invaluable resource, where you can exchange tips and feedback with your fellow makers, as well as share triumphs and disasters.

Please also feel free to follow @thehomefragranceworkbooks on Instagram for inspiration and related updates.

We are all part of a community

Why not support your fellow wax melt-makers? Learning to make melts is a personal choice and the end result is a product of love, time, expense and effort. Showing – then selling - that product to others is the next brave step. Be kind and helpful, and pay it forward.

Enjoy the journey.

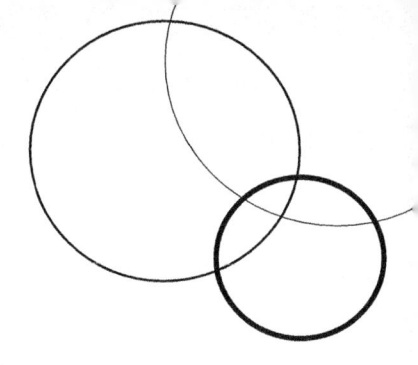

Part 1:

Getting Started

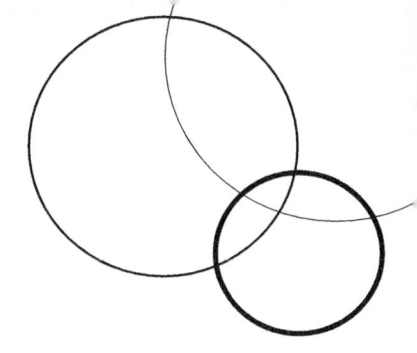

Part 1: Getting Started

1.1 What is a wax melt?

A wax melt is a product used to fragrance a room. Together with candles, diffusers and potpourri, it is part of the home fragrance family. Place a wax melt into the plate of a tealight or electric burner, wait for the heat generated by the burner to melt the wax, and for the liquid wax to release its fragrance into the air.

The wax melts sold in supermarkets and high street shops are, in the main, made from paraffin. These waxes are used by the mainstream companies because they are cheaper and consistently perform better than plant-based waxes. This book will go through the different types of waxes to help you decide which one to use.

1.2 Why make wax melts?

Wax melt-making is fun! And with Instagram, Facebook and Etsy all packed with people showing – and selling – their handmade waxy wares, you likely want to be part of the ever-growing homemade wax- melt industry.

There are twelve projects in Part 3 for you to try. Each of these projects uses shapes and formats that are popular with customers. To start, you will learn how to make the snap bars and deli pots. And because wax-melt customers love to have a wide selection of melts to choose from, advanced projects such as scoopable wax and wax crumble are also included.

1.3 Do you want to start selling?

Once you have spent time and money in making and testing your melts, you may feel ready to take the next step of selling them.

There is a lot to consider, because once you place a product for sale in the public domain, certain legislation will apply. Parts 4 and 5 take you through the steps needed to start your very own wax-melt business.

1.4 Safety precautions

Safety is an essential part of the wax melt-making process. You will be handling chemicals and other materials that can stain, damage and irritate the skin and eyes and are even fatal if swallowed. You will also be using equipment to melt and pour hot liquids. You must therefore protect yourself and others during the process.

The UK government has produced guidance about protecting your and others' health during the handling of hazardous substances, called 'Control of Substances Hazardous to Health' (also known as 'COSHH'): http://www.hse.gov.uk/coshh/index.htm

The guidance refers to using Personal Protective Equipment (PPE), so familiarise yourself with what you will need. If you do not wish to follow government guidance, at least have the following:

1. **Gloves**: Wear protective gloves when handling fragrance oils and wax, as well as during melting and pouring. An internet search can recommend the most suitable ones to protect against hot and corrosive spillages. Disposable gloves are a start, but you should double them up to provide some sort of barrier should you spill fragrance oil or liquid dye on your hands. Thick washing-up gloves are another option.

2. **Apron**: Wear an apron to protect your clothes from liquid wax spillages and dye splashes.

3. **Protective mask**: Some fragrance oils smell strong from the bottle, even more so once combined with hot wax. Some also cause headaches and dizziness. I work with a peppermint fragrance oil which takes my breath away with just one whiff, so I wear a mask while using it. A quick online search using the terms 'dust mask', or 'pollution mask' will yield suitable masks to buy. Look for those which are FFP2 or FFP3-rated.

4. **Shield or cordon off food preparation areas**: Unless you are lucky enough to have a dedicated workshop, most of us use our kitchens to make wax melts. Protect surfaces with newspaper, foil, or other barrier, and store all of your materials and equipment away from food and drink. Contamination is a risk and can be fatal.

5. **Keep supplies and equipment away from children and pets**: Make sure everything you use and work with is out of reach from children and pets. Fragrance oils, dyes and glitters are easily spilled or swallowed, which can be fatal.

Keep your materials and equipment in childproof storage, and hot liquid wax far out of reach from inquisitive hands, noses and paws.

6. **Suitable storage**: Fragrance oils, dyes and wax all react to both hot and very cold conditions, so find a suitable place to store them. Somewhere constantly dark and cool (perhaps a cellar?) will ensure your materials are not affected by the extremes of light and heat.

7. **Wash your hands**: It is good practice to thoroughly wash your hands after handling your supplies and equipment. Fragrance oils tend to remain on your hands and may cause irritation, so give your hands a good thorough clean!

1.5 Safety Data Sheets

I cannot emphasise this enough: **fragrance oils are chemicals and should be treated as such.**

Every fragrance oil has a corresponding Safety Data Sheet or 'SDS' (also called a Master Safety Data Sheet, or 'MSDS'), which is usually available at point-of-sale from suppliers. Split into various — usually sixteen — sections, the SDS provides basic information including supplier details, along with more in-depth information such as the chemical composition of the fragrance oil.

The SDS also lists all the hazards associated with using the fragrance oil (due to its composition) and the precautions to take when handling and making with it.

The following are some extracts from an SDS for a fragrance oil called 'Bubblegum'. Have a look through the sections to familiarise yourself with the layout and pertinent information.

SAFETY DATA SHEET

In accordance with REACH Regulation EC No.1907/2006

Product: Bubblegum Fragrance Oil 103479
Version: 1 Issue date: 01/06/2021

Section 1. Identification of the substance or the mixture and of the supplier

Product Identifier: Bubblegum Fragrance Oil 103479

(Contains:3 and 4-(4-Hydroxy-4-methylpentyl)-3- cyclohexene-1-carboxaldehyde, Linalyl acetate, alpha-Amylcinnamaldehyde, p-t-Butyl-alphamethylhydrocinnamic aldehyde)

Section 2. Hazards identification

Class and category of danger: Sensitisation - Skin Category 1

Hazardous to the Aquatic Environment - Acute Hazard Category 1

Hazardous to the Aquatic Environment - Long-term Hazard Category 1

H317, May cause an allergic skin reaction.

H410, Very toxic to aquatic life with long lasting effects.

Section 6. Accidental release measures

6.2 Environmental precautions: Keep away from drains, surface and ground water, and soil.

6.3 Methods and material for containment and cleaning up: Remove ignition sources. Provide adequate ventilation. Avoid excessive inhalation of vapours. Contain spillage immediately by use of sand or inert powder. Dispose of according to local regulations.

Section 7. Handling and storage

7.1 Precautions for safe handling: Keep away from heat, sparks, open flames and hot surfaces. – No smoking. Use personal protective equipment as required. Use in accordance with good manufacturing and industrial hygiene practices. Use in areas with adequate ventilation. Do not eat, drink or smoke when using this product.

Section 8. Exposure controls/personal protection

8.1 Exposure Controls Eye / Skin Protection

Wear protective gloves/eye protection/face protection

Respiratory Protection

a) Increase ventilation of the area with local exhaust ventilation.

b) Personnel can use an approved, appropriately fitted respirator with organic vapour cartridge or canisters and particulate filters.

Section 9. Disposal

Dispose of container and contents in accordance with local regulations.

Section 16. Other information

Product: Bubblegum Fragrance Oil 103479
Version: 1

Abbreviation	Meaning
Acute Tox. 4	Acute Toxicity - Oral Category 4
Aquatic Acute 1	Hazardous to the Aquatic Environment - Acute Hazard Category 1
Eye Dam. 1	Eye Damage / Irritation Category 1
H226 F	Flammable liquid and vapour.
H302	Harmful if swallowed.
H317	May cause an allergic skin reaction.
H400	Very toxic to aquatic life.
P202	Do not handle until all safety precautions have been read and understood.
P233	Keep container tightly closed.
P264	Wash hands and other contacted skin thoroughly after handling.
P270	Do not eat, drink or smoke when using this product.
P280	Wear protective gloves/eye protection/face protection.
P301/310	IF SWALLOWED: Immediately call a POISON CENTRE or doctor/physician.
P302/352	IF ON SKIN: Wash with plenty of soap and water.
P333/313	If skin irritation or rash occurs: Get medical advice/attention.
P370/378	In case of fire: Use carbon dioxide, dry chemical, foam for extinction.

Things to think about:

What hazards exist while you use this oil?

What precautions should you take to protect yourself and others?

Are these limited to times when you are handling the oil or at any other times?

What actions should you take to reduce the risk of any injury or damage?

If you have any fragrance oils to hand, have a look at their bottles – and their corresponding Safety Data Sheets – and apply what you have learnt so far. Identify the hazards and precautions, and see if you can relate these to the CLP labelling that is required for your melts once you start to sell them (s4.3).

Further reading:

https://www.hse.gov.uk/coshh/faq.htm#safety-data-sheets

1.6 Disposing of unwanted materials

When you start making wax melts you will accumulate a lot of spare materials like waxes and fragrance oils. Consider donating or selling your unwanted supplies to fellow makers. The various 'destash' groups on Facebook are a good starting point, as is Ebay and other online shopping platforms.

Fragrance oils that you are unable to sell should be disposed of appropriately, as detailed in their corresponding Safety Data Sheets.

1.7 Disposing of used wax melts

After all your testing you will likely have accumulated a lot of wax-melt build up in your burner! Keep your burner clean and ready for its next melt by removing the used melts on a regular basis.

The two most popular methods for removal are:

1. Refrigeration: Place the burner plate containing the melted wax into the fridge to harden for a few hours. The wax will then pop – or slide – out of the burner easily.

2. While the wax is still warm: Because the wax is still soft – but no longer hot to the touch – you can easily wipe it out from the burner using kitchen roll.

Used wax melts should be disposed of with the household rubbish and never in drains, sinks, or toilets.

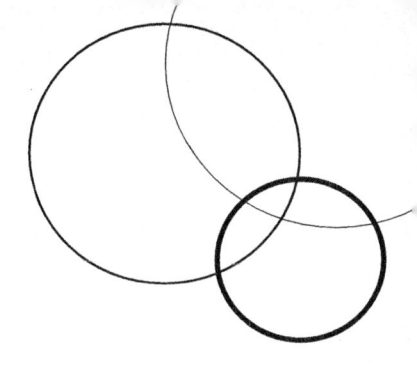

Part 2:

Materials and equipment

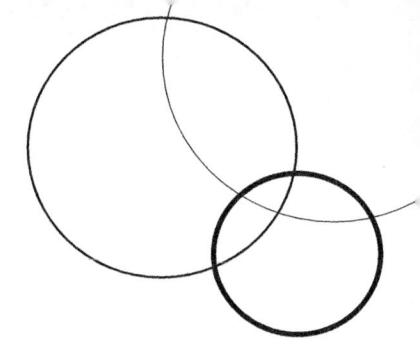

Part 2: Materials and equipment

As you go through this part of the book, you can use **Worksheet 1: Supplies List** to compile a 'shopping list' of the materials and equipment you need. Don't forget to have a look at the various supplies available from the **Suppliers** too.

Once you start testing and making the **Projects** in Part 3, use **Worksheet 2: Wax Testing Record** to note down all of your testing.

Essential materials for making wax melts:

- Wax(es)
- Moulds (silicone, plastic)
- Containers (deli pots, clamshells)
- Packaging
- Labels
- Fragrance oils
- Colours (liquid dye, mica)
- Decorations (glitter, botanicals)

2.1 Waxes

Plant-based waxes, paraffin waxes and blends therof are all used to make wax melts, and if you plan on making different *types* of melts, you will need a variety of waxes.

Start by testing out the smallest-size packs of different waxes (the 1kg size is usually sufficient).

Your choice of wax depends on the following:

- **Quality**: A good quality wax will have both good cold and hot throw. This means it will hold fragrance well even when it is not being used ('cold throw') and distribute that fragrance nicely when it is being used ('hot throw'). It will also need to hold dyes properly, and keep for several months without scent or colour fade. With some waxes, fragrance throw improves over time.

- **Ease of use**: A wax that doesn't need cutting into before measuring is helpful for the less mobile. Plus it saves time.

- **Value for money**: A good quality wax is one which performs consistently, i.e. most, if not all, fragrance oils work well with it. If you find yourself constantly changing wax to suit oils or dyes, reconsider your wax. You will save money and avoid stress in the long term.

- **Time spent making**: Some waxes take longer to cure than others, which will affect how long you (and your customers) have to wait before using your melts. And if you want to create your own wax blend, doing this successfully also takes time.

Once you find your winning formula: stick with it!

2.2 Paraffin Waxes

Known as 'mineral waxes', paraffin waxes are derived from petroleum, which is drilled from the ground, then refined.

Paraffin waxes are generally cheaper to buy than the plant-based ones and consistently give a better cold and hot throw. This means you will not have to do as much research or testing as with other waxes. If you are going into bigger scale production, paraffin waxes – and even para-wax combinations – will be a very economical material to use. Paraffin waxes usually come in pellet or block form.

Other advantages of paraffin waxes

- Able to hold large percentages of fragrance oil (known as a 'high fragrance load') for a stronger and longer-lasting scent throw

- Odour-free

- Dyes disperse easily so show up more vividly in the end product

- Cheaper than plant-based waxes.

Disadvantages

- Gets negative press compared with the plant-based waxes

- May require an additive to improve scent throw or appearance.

What paraffin users say

I talked with a number of wax melt makers about their wax preferences. One paraffin convert said the following:

"I moved to paraffin from soy. It can be challenging to find the correct temperatures required for each step of heating, combining fragrance and pouring but I find it a far superior wax for hot throw."

Popular paraffin waxes to try:

Kerax 4600

Sasol 6243 (a paraffin and stearin blend)

2.3 Plant-based Waxes

Plant-based waxes are made from sources such as soy, rapeseed and coconut. They are also known as 'natural' or 'vegetable' waxes.

They come in block, flake or pellet form. I have used a plant-based wax that came in powder form, and while it was tricky to handle (word of advice: don't sneeze while holding a scoop of powdered wax!), at least I did not have to prepare it by cutting beforehand.

Other advantages of plant-based waxes

- Have an attractive creamy appearance if poured and cooled correctly
- Tend to be marketed as 'natural' and 'eco-friendly'
- The majority of makers use plant-based waxes to make melts, so there is more information and reviews available

Disadvantages

- More expensive than paraffin waxes

- Plant-based waxes perform poorly if the fragrance load is inadequate or excessive, so additives and further testing will be required

- Some plant-based waxes do not 'take' well with dyes, particularly black and neon. Colours may appear too light or not combine properly.

What plant-based wax users say

Soy wax was by far the most popular plant-based wax amongst the wax melt makers I spoke to for this book. A number of them had the following to say about using soy waxes:

"Soy takes on my scents well, and gives a glossy finish especially when using botanicals. I find it also gives me an exceptional cold and hot throw".

"If anyone were to ask what wax I would recommend for a beginner, it would most definitely be soy. I find soy wax more forgiving and easier to work with."

One maker also said:

"After using soy waxes for several years I am now very tempted to use paraffin instead. One soy wax in particular emits a undesirable fatty odour when melting and after curing, and I do not want to have to discard my stock each time this occurs".

Popular plant-based waxes to try:

Kerax Kerasoy Pillar (soy)

Ecosystem RCX Melt Blend (a coconut and rapeseed oil blend)

2.4 Cure times

All waxes need to cure after pouring, regardless of type. Curing gives the mixture time to harden and disperses the fragrance evenly through the wax the longer it cures for.

Cure times depend on the type of wax and the amount of fragrance oil you have used. Generally speaking, paraffin waxes cure within a couple of days, while plant-based waxes need to cure for an average of two weeks before decent cold and hot throws are achieved.

Testing and research is the only way to determine the most effective cure times for your products.

Bear in mind that the more fragrance or base oil you use in the mixture, the softer the resulting wax melt, so if you are making products such as scoopable wax, the mixture will not – and should not – fully harden anyway.

Cure your melts away from draughts and direct sunlight, and out of reach of children and pets.

2.5 The 'natural' wax debate

Online forums are full of wax melt makers discussing their reasons for using paraffin instead of plant-based waxes, and vice versa. Choices are influenced by a number of factors including how the waxes are marketed as well as how the media reports on them.

Ensure that you are well informed before advertising the 'natural' virtues of your wax melts. Customers are savvier these days about the eco-credentials of the products they use, so it is worth preparing yourself for any questions that they may ask. You may want to include the information on your website (as a FAQ) or on your packaging.

Wax melt makers who use waxes like soy or beeswax may choose to market their wax melts as 'natural', 'non-toxic', or 'eco-friendly'. Using this kind of terminology to market a product is fine, but only if it is factually correct. There is a lot of research to do before you can make such a claim for your final product.

This kind of description tends to divide wax melt makers into being either 'good' or 'bad'. By saying your melts are 'natural' reflects negatively on those who use paraffin waxes, as it (intentionally or not) indicates that their paraffin-based products are inferior and bad for the environment. As you have read earlier in this Part, paraffin waxes are surprisingly superior in a number of ways compared to the plant-based ones!

Research the wax-making processes

It is worth researching the manufacturing processes that your wax undergoes before it reaches you. Some wax suppliers are forthcoming about how their waxes are made and provide all you need to know about the various processes on their websites.

Look at the origin of the wax. If it is plant-based, find out if the plant source is sustainably grown, how well the farmers are paid and whether farming and processing the crop damages local wildlife or waterways. If the wax is paraffin, research how it is extracted and processed and whether such processes damage the surrounding environment.

You can also find out how the wax is transported. If it is not grown or processed in your country, then it had to travel some distance (and most likely in fume-emitting transportation) to reach you.

The final product

If your wax is sustainably farmed, processed and transported without causing any harm whatsoever to the environment, by all means tell your customers about the virtues of this wax (and also tell me because I would love to buy it!).

However, it does not make sense to describe your wax melts as 'natural' if you then add chemical dyes and/or laboratory-made fragrances to it. As you know from reading about Safety Data Sheets in Part 1, the vast majority of fragrance oils are harmful or toxic to the environment, so to describe your final product as 'eco-friendly' may be construed as inaccurate and misleading.

Use factually correct terminology in your descriptions

One way to get around the 'eco-friendly' or 'natural' tag is simply by using factually correct terminology in your descriptions. Is the wax you use made from sustainable vegetation? Say so! You can say your melts are "Made using wax from sustainable resources," for example. This would be a correct statement. Is your wax made in the UK, so there are less fuel emissions compared to those waxes shipped over from the USA? Proudly inform customers that the wax you have used to make the wax melt is "Made in the UK".

Things to think about:

What waxes appeal to you and why?

Would you promote the benefits of your chosen wax(es) as a selling point? If so, how would you do this?

2.6 Wax melt formats, moulds and containers

Consider these factors when deciding which formats to sell:

Popularity amongst customers

Some customers like small shapes and sizes that are easy to 'snap and pop' into their burner, others enjoy cutting into or scooping wax out of jars. Start by making the three most popular melt formats (at the time of writing, these were hearts, bars and deli pots), then as your customer base – and confidence in making – grows, make other formats such as brittle and scoopable wax melts.

Shapes or containers?

Melts made using moulds will require removal from those moulds. If you make melts in bulk, un-moulding shapes takes time – and space! – compared with those melts which are poured straight into containers such as deli pots.

Price point

Moulds and packaging vary in price depending on where you purchase them, and whether you buy them in bulk. Moulds can also be reused time and time again, whereas containers need to be purchased each time.

Rarity

Some moulds are only available overseas, so are rare for UK customers. Get your hands on some and your melts will stand out in a market that is saturated with heart shapes.

2.7 Silicone moulds

Silicone moulds come in all sorts of fun shapes and sizes; donuts, mini cakes, stars, hearts, bars, even pineapples!

They are readily available online and in shops. Have a look in bargain shops for cheap silicone ice cube moulds, and on Ebay and Amazon for bundle deals. Silicone moulds are usually made for chocolate making and baking, so also check shops such as Lakeland.

Wax is easily removed from silicone moulds, since the mould is made from a soft and flexible material.

Silicone moulds are also easy to clean and reuse. I scrub mine with a cheap plastic washing up brush and dishwashing liquid. Other makers clean their moulds in the dishwasher or washing machine – with a capful of detergent – to clean theirs, although before you do this, do check the washing advice on the mould packaging beforehand.

Be aware of the Food Imitation Regulations when making with moulds designed for food use. See Part 4 for more information.

2.8 Plastic moulds

If you decide to use a plastic mould, you will need to find a wax that can slide or 'pop' out easily from it. Because they are set into sheets, plastic moulds are less flexible than silicone ones, so unless you conduct some testing, you may find that your wax will not easily release from the mould, or that it comes out crumbly. Personally I prefer silicone to plastic, while other melt makers happily switch between the two.

You can also design your own plastic mould, so your melts will be totally unique to you. Incorporate your logo onto them, create a slogan, anything goes!

2.9 Container melts

If you prefer containers for your wax melts, plastic 'deli pots' (that's right, the very same that your takeaway uses for sauces) and 'clamshells' are the standard.

Deli pots are available in a number of sizes from 1 ounce to 16 ounces, with 2 ounce being the most commonly used for wax melts. 1 ounce pots generally hold around 25g of wax, but always weigh the finished melt yourself to make sure, as pot styles do vary. These types of melts are also known as 'wax pots' and 'wax shots'.

Clamshells are so-called because the wax is held between two pieces of plastic sheeting, which open up like a clam. They come in cube format (single cube, duo slabs, four cubes, six cubes, and so on), although I have also seen clamshell hearts, clamshell bars and clamshell 'wheels', all of which look very pretty when more than one colour is poured into them.

Wax is usually segmented in clamshells, so you can simply pop a piece of wax straight out of the container into the burner plate.

These container melts are easy to send in the mail as they lie flat and the packaging more or less protects them during transit. More often than not the packaging is also recyclable, which will appeal to the eco-conscious customer. There is also an advantage for you in making this type of melt as you won't have to spend time unmoulding the wax from moulds.

2.10 Creative melt formats

Customers are now demanding more from their wax melts. It is not enough for them to smell good and look good, they have to be fun to use too. In addition to shapes and containers, there are a number of other formats to cater for this demand.

Squeezable wax tubes, anyone? Or how about wax that you scoop out like ice cream?

Check out Projects 5 to 9 in Part 3 to learn how to make some of them!

Wax brittle is wax that has been poured onto a flat surface (like a tray, for example), then decorated with more wax and glitter. Once it has hardened, the wax 'slab' is broken up into pieces. Also known as 'wax shards' or 'snappable wax'.

Wax crumble is wax that has been 'scraped through' while it is cooling, resulting in balls of wax crumbs. Crumble looks great if you make the same scent in more than one colour.

Scoopable wax is made using a combination of oil and wax. The resulting wax is soft, with a balm-like texture, which can be 'scooped' out like ice cream. Also known as 'scoopies', or 'butter'.

Squeezable wax is also made with a combination of oil and wax, but the ratio of oil is higher than that used in scoopable wax. The resulting wax is almost purely liquid in texture, and is squeezed out like paint. Also known as 'liquid wax' or 'wax cream'.

Wax pies can be made using scoopable wax, often with different coloured layers poured on top of each other. Wax pies can also be made with the normal, harder wax so you tip them out of their containers to chop up or grate (which some customers enjoy doing).

Beware of using food-like connotations to describe and/or name any wax products that you sell. Read more about Food Imitation in Part 4.

2.11 Wax melt packaging

If you are selling individually shaped melts, put them into packaging that will attract customers. Here are some ideas for packaging the smaller shaped melts such as hearts and brittle pieces.

Cellophane bags are an excellent choice as customers can easily see what scents and shapes they are buying. Available in a variety of dimensions, there is a cellophane bag to suit every melt shape and size.

Sweetie and glassine bags (made of paper or waxed paper) are not transparent like cellophane bags but are inexpensive and come in a wide variety of colours and designs.

Pouches (like those used for coffee) are available with or without a see-through panel, and come in a variety of finishes including kraft and metallic. They are pleasant to hold, and if you get the gusseted type, stand upright, which is useful for display purposes.

Plastic jars and tubs are handy for smaller sized melts, and since they are clear, your melts – especially if they are all different colours – will look very appealing while on display.

Lidded tins are another appealing way to store melts. Consider using tissue paper to line the tins and cover the melts for a 'high end' look.

Tissue paper is an eco-friendly way to package melts. Seal them up with twine and a logo sticker for a neat, natural look. Also consider having your logo or business name printed onto the tissue paper for a professional finish.

2.12 Labelling your wax melts

It is standard practice to have the business name, logo and the melt name/scent printed onto a label that is attached to the front of the wax melt packaging. A label with the CLP information (see Part 4 for more about CLP) and key business details is then attached to the back of the packaging.

You may find it helpful – and reassuring – to check with your local Trading Standards office that they are satisfied with your labelling. Some offices demand that a full address be included, while others are happy with a website and email address. You will not know until you check.

Below is an example of labelling for the front and back of your wax melt packaging.

Label for front

(Your logo if you have one)

Flora Wax Company

DAFFODIL

Scented Wax Melts

Label for back

Name of melt

CLP information, pictograms

Usage information

Business contact details/website

2.13 Fragrance oils

You must also decide on your fragrances. For me this is definitely the most fun (but costly) part of making wax melts, as I just have to try them all!

Fragrance oils are 100% concentrated, so use them carefully and safely (see sections 1.4 and 1.5 for more information).

They are added to the melted wax before being poured into the container or mould, and usually at the same time as dye. There is a recommended temperature at which you add the fragrance oil to wax, and this depends on the type of wax you are using. Temperatures range from 40 degrees Celsius to 85 degrees Celsius, so you will need to check the information provided by the wax supplier for best results.

You will need to test how much fragrance oil to use when making melts. Known as 'fragrance load', the amount of fragrance oil required depends on a number of factors (wax type and IFRA recommendation being the main ones). Using a 10% fragrance oil load in wax is a good starting point, not just because it is the standard used by most makers, but also because it is easier to calculate further batches by the number 10! By testing at a set percentage – such as 10% – you can determine whether or not you need to adjust the percentage for future batches, should the resulting fragrance be too strong or weak.

Make sure to use consistent measurements for your wax, fragrance and dyes; weigh everything using the same units of measurement. I weigh all of my solid materials in grams.

2.14 Calculating fragrance load

For every 100g of wax you measure out, measure out 10g of fragrance oil. This is known as 10% 'fragrance load'. So if you use 200g wax, you will need to measure 20g of fragrance oil. This will still be a 10% fragrance load. If the resulting melt smells too strong at this percentage, lower the fragrance load to 6%. So for every 100g of wax used, use 6g of fragrance oil. Adjust further as necessary.

Most CLP labelling provided by suppliers is for fragrance loads of up to 10%. If you use more than this, you will need a different CLP label for the higher fragrance load. See Part 4 for more information about CLP.

2.15 Fragrance families

Which fragrances will you start with?

Choose at least one oil from the following fragrance families:

- Fruity: for example apple, lemon, watermelon, strawberry

- Bakery: for example cake, cookies, gingerbread

- Floral: for example rose, lavender, jasmine

- Duplicates: for example those 'inspired by' designer perfumes, bath and body brands, popular laundry and cleaning products.

I find looking at the fragrance oils on a supplier's website a great starting point, as suppliers often group their fragrance oils into categories like those used above. Read the product descriptions and reviews to get a better idea of how the oil performs in the different types of wax and its popularity with melt makers and their customers.

2.16 Fragrance themes and collections

When I was selling wax melts I found that grouping wax melts into ready-to-buy collections was popular, as customers enjoy collecting the different scents, especially if they are themed.

Here are some ideas you can use with your melts, to get those customers buying!

Matching your moulds to your fragrances

If you have a snowman scented mould, why not use a snowman-type scent? Something cool and refreshing, like mint or lemon.

I have also seen flower shaped silicone moulds that will go well together with a range of floral fragrance oils; how about a Spring Garden collection?

Duplicate – or 'dupe' – collections

A set of laundry product-scented melts will be popular with customers who like clean, soapy fragrances. And how about designer perfume melts? Perfect for those who like the smell of luxury!

Seasonal collections

A summer collection will be popular when the temperature rises. Melts that smell like sun lotion, the beach, even a cocktail or two, are guaranteed crowd-pleasers.

Subscription boxes

With these, customers sign up to receive a themed box from you every month. These require dedication as you need to come up with a theme for each month, then make and/or find other goodies that also suit the theme to include in the box.

Character and film-inspired collections

I have made wax melt collections inspired by unicorns, mermaids, Willy Wonka, even the Wizard of Oz! Find fragrances that you think suit the general style of the collection you are making and throw a 'wild card' fragrance in there too, to spice things up. For my Wizard of Oz collection, I made yellow bricks (as in the Yellow Brick Road) using a peppermint fragrance oil, bright yellow dye and a silicone block mould. Use your imagination!

If you decide to make a character or film-inspired collection, for legal reasons you cannot use images, fonts or any other designs from the actual character or film. This applies both to your product itself and any advertising/promotion you do. See Part 4 for more information about intellectual property rights.

2.17 Essential oils

Using essential oils in wax melts is an option, albeit an expensive one. Essential oils are extracted directly from plant materials (unlike fragrance oils which are synthetic) and the cost of this process is reflected in the price.

They are also more potent and toxic, so essential oils are not recommended for use during pregnancy or around pets, and may trigger sensitivities in users. Make sure you research this option thoroughly.

I personally love the idea of scenting my home with essential oils as it is so easy to just pop a melt into a burner and feel the positive effects within minutes as you inhale the scent.

If you want to make melts using essential oils, try Project 10 in Part 3.

Case Study: Melt Me Real Good

www.meltmerealgood.co.uk

Alice Naylor is the artisan behind Melt Me Real Good, a business she started after leaving paid employment and moving to Scotland during the coronavirus pandemic. Just one year after making melts as a hobby, Alice has established a loyal customer base and also supplies a number of shops. Her range includes wax melts made using essential oils, an option she would not have usually considered:

"A friend of mine swore by the positive effects that essential oils had on her well-being and suggested I make some wax melts incorporating them, but I was worried that these would be too niche for my still-growing customer base. I was also worried about the price difference compared with fragrance oils.

I did identify the need to stand out from other wax melt businesses, however, so after extensive research I trialled three blended oils, all with different properties, in melts. They proved very popular, and one customer specifically uses them during the crystal therapy sessions she runs. Her clients always comment on how relaxing and soothing the scents are.

I do advise taking the time to research this area carefully, however, as the oils are much stronger than fragrance oils. I tested for a long time before finding the right balance of oil and wax. Essential oils are definitely something to consider, though, as they smell amazing and have so many therapeutic qualities. There is a lot of fun to be had too!"

* * *

2.18 Colours and decorations

The combination of wax and fragrance oil generally sets to a creamy white shade. You can enhance the appeal of your melts by colouring and decorating them. Not only does colouring your melts make them visually attractive, it also allows customers to differentiate between scents.

You may choose to keep the creamy colour and not add any dyes. A number of melt makers choose to sell their melts this way and these are known as 'naked' melts. Because they have no additional dyes, customers perceive the melts as 'natural' and more 'eco-friendly'; the natural wax debate rages on!

Using no colour or decoration also means less expense for you and less time spent using dyes to create special effects. It is up to you which option you go for!

2.19 Dyes

Dyes come in liquid, chip/flake and powder form.

Liquid dyes typically come in small bottles with a dropper-style cap, so you simply squeeze the dye into the melted wax, drop by drop. The more drops you use, the more intense the final colour. Your supplier will have a shade chart for each colour, showing how much dye to use to achieve the desired shade. You can also combine dyes to make new colours.

A good comprehensive set of liquid dyes to have includes the colours red, blue, yellow, green, pink, purple, orange, brown and black.

Carefully add the colour while the wax is hot, so you can stir it thoroughly and evenly through the wax. Most makers add the colour at the same time as fragrance.

You will need to wear gloves and an apron when working with liquid dyes as the colour is extremely concentrated and therefore very difficult to remove should you spill some on your skin or clothing.

Chip and flake dyes are far less messy to use, as you simply sprinkle a few flakes at a time into the wax and stir. Dye chips will need weighing (follow the supplier's instructions) to achieve a colour match. As with liquid dyes, you can combine chips/flakes to make new colours.

Marbling is another way to colour wax melts and results in a very attractive effect that I call the 'Swirl-And-Dot' technique. It involves swirling and dotting at least one colour into wax, creating a 'marbled' effect. If you have ever marbled paper, the effect is the same. I recommend using a medium-large sized mould or container when marbling, as it is very fiddly doing it in smaller shapes; it is also helpful to see the colours properly during the process. Your wax will need to be fully liquid and hot and you must work quickly, before the wax starts setting.

Project 3 in Part 3 takes you through marbling.

2.20 Mica

Mica is another product you can use to colour and decorate wax melts. It also gives a beautiful shimmer effect while melting, so is very popular amongst those makers and customers who like to share videos of their melts in action.

Mica is supplied as a powder so needs careful handling and storage to prevent spillages. Unless you take the mica out using a scoop, you will need to wear gloves to prevent the mica from attaching itself to your fingers and anything else you touch from that point onwards!

Use just a pinch of mica at first, adding more if needed. Stir it thoroughly into the hot wax and be careful not to add too much as it will stiffen the wax mixture, making it difficult to pour.

Mica can be used in two ways. Use it to fully colour your melts (as with the liquid dyes), or to 'paint' the surface of your melts. The latter is a good method to enhance any smaller details that your melts may have, such as lettering or facial details.

If you are fully colouring your melts with mica, add it to your wax while it is completely liquid and hot, ensuring it is stirred in thoroughly so the colour is distributed without any lumps.

If you are painting with mica, wait until your melts have set before decorating. Wet a brush which has a small applicator (such as an eyeliner brush or mini paintbrush), dip into the mica and apply to your melt. Very skilled makers can create works of art using mica this way; have a go and see what you can do!

An attractive effect to try in wax melt-making is the ombre effect, where two or more colours look as if they have seamlessly merged into each other. You can achieve this effect using liquid and chip dyes as well as mica.

To make an ombre effect with mica in your melts, try Project 4 in Part 3.

2.21 Glitter

Glitter adds an eye-catching sparkle to wax melts and comes in fine and chunky sizes. There are many colours and mixes available, and the chunky versions may also feature small shapes such as hearts and stars.

Because they are flammable, craft glitter and sequins are not suitable for use in melts, so make sure you use glitter that is deemed suitable for use in wax melts.

Biodegradable glitter (eucalyptus being the main source) is

becoming more readily available from a number of suppliers, although it is more expensive than standard glitter (in some cases, twice as much). Biodegradable glitter attracts eco-conscious customers, so if you use it, promote this fact.

To use glitter with container melts, simply sprinkle some over the top of your melt after you have poured it, but before it sets fully. Glitter needs something to stick – but not sink in – to.

To use glitter with moulds, sprinkle the glitter into the mould before pouring the wax in.

2.22 Other decorations

Melts can be decorated with other items too. I have seen melts that incorporate chunks of crystals, resin figurines and even collectable metal charms. If you use solid decorations such as crystals and charms to decorate your melts, inform your customers that these items must be removed before melting as they can pose a fire risk.

Dried flowers and other plant parts can be used to decorate melts and look especially good in hanging wax tablets. Cinnamon sticks, rose petals and lavender flowers make lovely decorations and you can use the corresponding fragrance oils to make them appealing to customers who like the 'natural' look. Project 10 in Part 3 is a technique that uses botanical elements in a hanging wax tablet.

Case Study: Ofina

www.ofinacandles.co.uk

Fiona Nottingham owns Ofina, a home-fragrance business which she set up after completing a candle-making course.

She knew she wanted a clean and simple look to her brand and carried this theme through to her wax melts. Fiona also tested for a whole year before finding a wax blend that cured to the finish she was after.

Her wax melts demonstrate that you do not always have to fully colour your melts for them to be eye catching. And if you do want to add colour, this can be done in other ways.

"I very seldom use colours as I like the 'purity' of the white colour you get once the wax has cured. I am happy to use colours, however, should a customer request it.

I mainly use botanicals to add colour and match these to the fragrances I use. Lavender flowers are great to use as a decoration on top of a lavender-scented wax melt, as are other botanicals like mint leaves or rosebuds."

Things to think about:

Which wax melt formats appeal to you? Do you think you could establish a customer base using these particular wax formats?

Which fragrances appeal to you? Do you think you could establish a specialist or a broader customer base using these particular fragrances?

Are you going to colour and/or decorate your melts? How much of your budget and your time will be spent on this?

What packaging do you need?

What labels do you need and how will you print them?

2.23 Equipment

To make wax melts, you need equipment for the following processes:

- Weighing
- Melting
- Pouring and stirring
- Protecting and cleaning up

A number of companies listed in the Suppliers section sell the majority of the equipment you need. I also recommend looking in catering shops for melting equipment and general homeware shops for cheap heatproof jugs and spoons.

Essential equipment for making wax melts:
- Table top scales
- Measuring cups
- Wax thermometer
- Wax melter (bain-marie, microwave)
- Jugs
- Spoons

2.24 Weighing

You need scales to weigh your wax, fragrance oils and dye chips. A plastic or metal scoop is also useful for handling wax that comes in flake or pellet form.

Try to distribute and weigh your supplies in separate containers; I use a set of plastic measuring cups bought online and each of the cups has a 'lip' which enables easy pouring.

Unless a supplier advises otherwise, weigh everything in grams. Traditional kitchen scales can be used to weigh your fragrance oils, dye and wax, although I prefer electronic scales as I have a small kitchen and their shape and size makes them easy to store away. Electronic scales can be bought relatively inexpensively.

2.25 Melting

A wax thermometer is essential for wax melt-making, as the various processes of melting, adding fragrance and pouring rely on having the wax at the correct temperature. I clip a chandler's thermometer to the inside of my bain-marie and you can do this too if you are using a saucepan or other wax-melting container to easily monitor the temperature of the wax.

You also need to decide how you are going to melt your wax. When I was first starting out I used a microwave to melt wax. I would put the wax into a microwaveable jug and heat it up in small increments (every fifteen seconds). This method became quite tiresome, as I had to check on the wax at frequent intervals, so I do not recommend microwaving as a long-term method.

Some crafters use the classic 'saucepan within a saucepan' technique, however, bain-maries are not that much more expensive and save a lot of hassle once you start making more melts. I love my bain-marie because it keeps the water hot throughout the day, meaning I can make melts in the morning, go off to do other things, then come back later to make more!

If you find yourself making hundreds of melts every week – or even every day – consider investing in a machine capable of handling bigger quantities of wax. A number of suppliers sell digitally controlled wax melting machines which make the whole process of melting and pouring much easier. Check the Suppliers section of this book as a starting point.

2.26 Pouring and stirring

Once the wax has melted, you will need a container in which to stir it and combine the dye and fragrance. I use one clear plastic heatproof jug per fragrance and stir with a wooden spoon; other makers prefer metal jugs and spoons.

2.27 Protection and cleaning up

Follow the safety precautions as outlined in Part 1 and any other guidance your supplier gives you.

Jugs, cups and spoons can all be wiped with paper towels then rinsed out. I use a delegated scrubbing brush and washing up liquid to clean my equipment and moulds.

Clean, empty fragrance bottles can usually be recycled. If you have unused bottles of oil and dye, you can give these to other crafters or dispose of them as instructed by your local council (not with your household rubbish or in any drains). Consult your council's environmental service on how to dispose of hazardous materials.

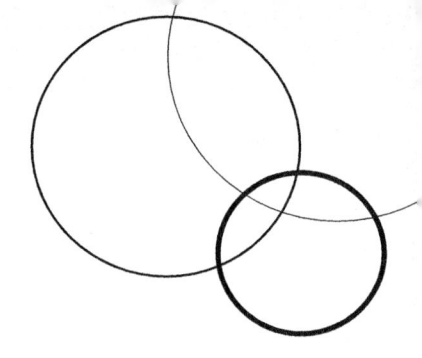

Part 3:

Projects

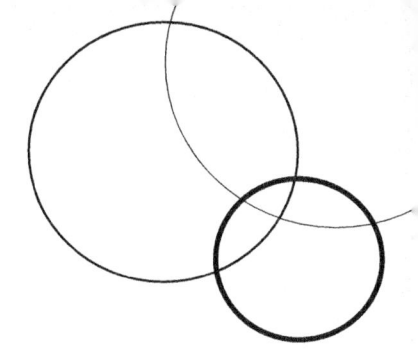

Part 3: Projects

The first two projects here teach you how to make two popular wax-melt formats: deli pot melts and heart shapes.

Project 1 uses no colours – just fragrance oils – so you get used to pouring hot wax into containers.

Project 2 introduces colour and will help you to judge how much colour to use each time you make melts.

Project 3 goes through the marbling effect using liquid dyes, which is a great way to showcase different colours and show off your decorating skills!

Project 4 teaches you how to achieve the ombre effect using mica powders.

Projects 5 and **6** combine the colouring and decorating of wax with two more wax formats: wax brittle and wax crumble.

Close monitoring of wax is required while making these types of melts and as you practise them, you will learn to identify the stage at which the wax can be worked with so you can pour that extra layer or create crumbles.

It is the oil component in **Projects 7, 8** and **9** that keep the wax soft and liquid for making scoopable and squeezable wax melts. If you find the resulting wax too soft for your liking, decrease the amount of base oil as necessary. And if you find the wax melt difficult to scoop or squeeze out, increase the amount of base oil. If you want to experiment further, try substituting coconut oil with mineral oil.

Projects 10, 11 and **12** are expansion projects, where you learn to make hanging wax tablets, simmering granules and mini diffusers. Consider adding these to your existing wax melt range and see if they are popular with your customers.

PROJECT 1: Deli pot wax melts

Materials

100g Wax

10g Fragrance oil of your choice

x2 40g (2 oz) Deli pots

Equipment

Jug

Wax thermometer

Wax melter (eg. bain-marie, microwave)

Spoon to stir the wax and oil together

Directions

1. Pour the wax into the wax melter (or other suitable container if using a microwave) and melt to the recommended temperature. Stir occasionally to ensure the wax is melting thoroughly. A good indicator of this is when it becomes completely clear.

2. Transfer the melted wax into the jug. Measure the wax temperature again to ensure it is the recommended temperature at which you can add the fragrance oil. Add the fragrance oil, stirring it thoroughly into the wax.

3. Measure the temperature of the mixture again, for the recommended pouring temperature. If you pour the mixture too hot, you may melt the container you are pouring into and/or the wax will form a 'dip' in the middle during the cooling process.

4. Slowly and carefully pour the mixture into the first deli pot, filling it up to the indented part of the pot. If you pour beyond this part, you will overfill the pot and the lid may not fit securely once the wax has cooled.

5. Now fill the second pot. You will likely have some wax left over, which you can dispose of with the household rubbish, however I recommend pouring this into a spare deli pot or silicone mould if you plan on selling. You can use these spares for quality checking purposes, so if there are any complaints with the batch, you can test the melt for yourself.

6. Leave the pots to cure for the recommended time and test the melts when ready.

PROJECT 2:
Heart shaped wax melts

Materials

100g Wax

10g Fragrance oil of your choice

2 drops of liquid dye of your choice (If you are using dye chips/flakes, have the recommended amount measured out)

Silicone hearts mould

Equipment

Jug

Wax thermometer

Wax melter (e.g. bain-marie, microwave)

Spoon to stir the wax, oil and dye together

Directions

1. Melt the wax and add fragrance oil as per steps 1 and 2 in Project 1. Add the dye, stirring it thoroughly into the wax, ensuring there are no lumps or streaks in the mixture.

2. Ensure the mixture has cooled to a suitable pouring temperature, then pour into each heart, filling to the top of each heart segment.

3. Leave to cure for the recommended time and test when ready.

PROJECT 3: Marbling effects

Materials

100g Wax

10g Fragrance oil of your choice

Medium sized container (try a deli pot)

2 drops of two different-coloured liquid dyes

1 cocktail stick or paperclip (bent straight) per dye colour

Equipment

Jug

Wax thermometer

Wax melter (e.g. bain-marie, microwave)

Spoon to stir the wax, oil and dye together

Directions

1. Melt your wax and add fragrance as per steps 1 and 2 in Project 1.

2. Pour the wax into the mould/container.

3. Dip one end of a cocktail stick/paperclip into the first of the liquid dye drops you have chosen. Now dip this end into the wax you have just poured out, 'swirling' the cocktail stick/paperclip through the wax and around the container. Try not to let the swirls go into each other, as this will simply colour the melt fully with the one colour, which is not the intended effect!

4. Dip the end of the second cocktail stick/paperclip into

the next colour you have chosen, 'swirling' as before. Create new swirls and/or 'dot' the end into the wax to add a touch of colour. As before, do not let the swirls fully merge into each other, as the colours will combine and look murky.

5. Leave the melt to cure for the recommended time.

Once cured, you will be able to see the effects all your 'swirling' and 'dotting' created, and decide whether or not you need more practice!

PROJECT 4: Ombre effects

Materials

100g Wax

10g Fragrance oil of your choice

Bar mould

Mica in 2 colours of your choice (try yellow and orange)

Equipment

Wax thermometer

Wax melter (e.g. bain-marie, microwave)

Two jugs

Two spoons

Directions

1. Melt the wax and add fragrance as per steps 1 and 2 in Project 1.

2. Divide the wax equally between the two jugs. Add one mica colour per jug, stirring the mica in thoroughly so there are no lumps and the colour is distributed evenly.

3. With the mould ready in front of you, hold a jug in each hand at opposite ends of the mould. Slowly pour the contents into the mould at the same time.

4. Once cured, you will be able to see whether your Duo-Pour technique was successful!

PROJECT 5: Wax brittle

Materials

200g Wax

20g Fragrance oil of your choice

Liquid dye or dye chips/flakes of your choice in 1 colour (try light purple)

Mica in 1 colour (try pink)

Glitter in 1 colour (try gold)

Small sized baking/oven tray

Equipment

Wax thermometer

Wax melter (e.g. bain-marie, microwave)

Spoon to stir the wax, oil and dye together

Two jugs

Two spoons

Directions

1. Melt the wax and add fragrance per steps 1 and 2 in Project 1.

2. Pour 50g of the mixture into one jug and set aside.

3. Add the dye into the main jug, stirring it thoroughly into the wax.

4. Add some mica to the melted wax in the other jug, adding a little at a time. If you use too little mica, the effect will

not be as dramatic. Too much mica, and the wax will clog up, becoming too thick to stir and pour.

5. Ensure the mixture in the main jug is at optimum pouring temperature, then pour all of the contents into the baking/oven tray.

6. Wait for at least ten minutes for the mixture to settle and cool, before you pour the contents of the other jug across it. Pour so that the wax comes out in a thin line, and 'drizzle' it across the tray, creating wavy lines, swirls, drips and dots.

7. Sprinkle some glitter evenly across the tray, ensuring it adheres to both mixtures.

8. Leave the wax to harden overnight and to cure for the recommended time.

9. Remove the wax from the tray. (You will find that wax slides out from baking/oven trays fairly easily if it has been left in a cool place to settle). You should now be holding a big slab of drizzled, decorated wax. Now comes the painful – or for some, therapeutic – part; breaking the slab into smaller pieces, thereby creating 'wax brittle' or 'wax shards'. Try not to break the pieces too small, or you will end up with flakes. Aim for 5cm-long pieces.

PROJECT 6: Wax Crumble

Materials

200g Wax

20g Fragrance oil of your choice (try rose)

Liquid dye or dye chips/flakes of your choice in 2 colours (try red and yellow)

2 small sized baking/oven trays

Equipment

Wax thermometer

Wax melter (e.g. bain-marie, microwave)

Two jugs

Two spoons

Fork

Directions

1. Melt the wax and add fragrance as per steps 1 and 2 in Project 1.
2. Divide the mixture evenly between two jugs.
3. Add one dye per jug and stir thoroughly.
4. Ensure the mixtures in both jugs are at optimum pouring temperature, then pour the contents of each jug into separate baking/oven trays, filling to the top where possible.
5. Wait for the mixtures to settle and cool, but not fully. You are looking for the point at which the wax has started to

settle but not hardened completely. Use a fork to test the consistency; the mixture should feel like sticky clay. When it has reached this point, scrape the fork through the wax, creating 'balls' of wax mixture in the tray. Do this until all the wax in both trays has been scraped through, forming wax 'crumbles'.

6. Repeat this process for the other mixture.

7. Leave both trays of crumbles to fully harden overnight.

8. Combine both crumbles into one tray, carefully mixing the different coloured crumbles together. This is so that, when you put the crumbles into packaging, the colours are evenly represented.

9. Cure the wax crumbles. Use a spoon or scoop to put them into packaging when they are ready.

PROJECT 7: Scoopable wax

Materials

First decide on a wax blend. I have included three of the most popular here. Choose from:

BLEND 1

A purely soy recipe, this consists of:

- 150g C3 wax
- 50g soybean oil

OR

BLEND 2

- 150g coconut oil
- 50g Golden Wax 494

OR

BLEND 3

- 175g C6 wax
- 25g coconut oil

20g Fragrance oil of your choice (try peppermint)

Liquid dye or dye chips/flakes of your choice in1 colour (try light teal)

Equipment

Wax thermometer

Wax melter (e.g. bain-marie, microwave)

Jug

Spoon

Lidded containers for the scoopable wax, e.g. jam jars x2

Directions

1. Melt the wax and add fragrance as per steps 1 and 2 in Project 1.
2. Add the dye and base oil, stirring the mixture thoroughly.
3. Slowly and carefully pour the mixture into the jars.
4. Cure the wax for the recommended time.
5. When ready to use, a small spoon or scoop can be used to remove the wax from the jar and put it into a burner.

PROJECT 8: Squeezable wax

Materials

50g C6 wax

150g coconut oil

20g Fragrance oil of your choice

Dye colour of your choice (try navy blue)

Glitter (try gold)

Equipment

Wax thermometer

Wax melter (e.g. bain-marie, microwave)

Jug

Spoon

Three small squeezy bottle containers with stoppers/caps

Funnel

Directions

1. Melt the wax and add fragrance as per steps 1 and 2 in Project 1.
2. Add the dye and stir thoroughly.
3. Sprinkle in glitter a little at a time, stirring thoroughly.
4. Slowly and carefully pour the mixture into each of the squeezy bottles, via the funnel.
5. Cure the wax for at least 48 hours and make sure to shake the bottle before every use.

PROJECT 9:
Layered scoopable wax pie

Materials

Choose one of the wax blends listed in Project 7

20g Fragrance oil of your choice (try candyfloss)

Liquid dye or dye chips/flakes, or mica in two colours of your choice (try pink and purple)

Glitter (try silver)

Equipment

Wax thermometer

Wax melter (e.g. bain-marie, microwave)

Two jugs

Two spoons

Lidded box, i.e. clear plastic takeaway box, with a halfway line marked out with ink

Directions

1. Melt the wax and add fragrance as per steps 1 and 2 in Project 1.

2. Divide the wax evenly between two jugs.

3. Now add one colour into each jug, stirring thoroughly.

4. Set aside one of the jugs for later. Keep this jug warm – such as in a bowl of hot water – so the wax does not harden.

5. Slowly pour the contents of the other jug into the container, up to the halfway line.

6. Wait at least one hour, for the wax to harden and cool.

7. Ensure the mixture in the jug you have put aside is hot and pourable. Slowly and carefully pour the mixture into the container, on top of the wax you poured earlier. Ensure that both layers are even in size.

8. Sprinkle glitter over the top of the wax, ensuring it sticks to – but does not sink into – the cooling wax.

9. Cure the wax for the recommended time.

10. A small spoon or scoop can be used to remove the wax from the container.

Once you have confidence in pouring layers, try adding more colours. Five will look fantastic, like a rainbow! Ensure you mark each layer on the outside of the container so you know when to stop pouring.

PROJECT 10:
Hanging wax tablets

Materials

100g Wax

10g essential (wax-suitable) oil - try orange or cinnamon (you can substitute this for fragrance oil if you wish)

Selection of whole and halved dried orange slices

Silicone mould, with four slab or bar segments

Strips of orange ribbon, cut into 10cm lengths

Equipment

Wax thermometer

Wax melter (e.g. bain-marie, microwave)

Spoon

Plastic jug

Metal skewer (or a mini circle-shaped cookie cutter, measuring 1cm in diameter)

Directions

1. Melt the wax and add fragrance as per steps 1 and 2 in Project 1.
2. Arrange one, two or three orange slices per segment in the mould.
3. Pour the mixture into each segment of the mould, covering the orange slices, and filling to the top.

4. Wait for the wax to semi-harden. You are looking for the stage at which it has changed to a creamy white colour and is soft enough to be indented or pierced through without breaking apart. If you are using a skewer, carefully pierce a hole into the top and centre of each slab, ensuring the holes you make are clearly defined and neat. Aim for a 1cm diameter, and make sure you do not pierce through the other side of the slab into the mould! If you are using a mini circle-shaped cookie cutter, carefully press it into the top of each slab, creating an indent.

5. Set the mould aside and leave to cure.

6. When the wax has fully cured, remove from the mould. Thread a length of ribbon through the holes at the top of each slab, tying the ends neatly.

There are other variations you can make with wax tablets. Try a relaxing lavender fragrance and real lavender flowers, or a lush rose fragrance oil complete with real red rose petals and buds. A summertime essential would be citronella oil (said to repel bugs and insects, complete with dried lemon slices). And don't forget to match the ribbon colour!

PROJECT 11: Simmering granules

Materials

100g dishwasher salts or salt chunks

5g fragrance oil (try lemon)

Liquid dye (try yellow)

Equipment

Large jar with screw lid

Directions

1. Place the salts into the jar. Add the fragrance oil and dye, a little at a time. Place the lid on top of the jar and shake the jar every time you add the oil and dye, so they are evenly distributed amongst the salts.

2. Give the jar a few more shakes, then screw the lid onto the jar. Store somewhere dark and cool for at least a week. Occasionally shake the jar to thoroughly combine the contents.

3. Test the salts in a wax melt burner (start with a teaspoon's worth). If you are happy with the hot throw, they are ready to use. Test their cold throw by placing at least two teaspoons' worth into a saucer or tray. Their scent should be detectable within half an hour if placed into a small space or room.

4. Store simmering granules in an airtight container away from direct sunlight when not in use. Remember to shake them occasionally and before each use.

PROJECT 12 : Mini diffusers

Materials

6ml Augeo diffuser base

1ml fragrance oil (try strawberry)

Half a drop of liquid diffuser dye (try bright pink)

Equipment

Mini hanging diffuser bottle (also known as a car diffuser) with a cork or wood inlaid cap

Measuring cup

Spoon

Funnel

Directions

1. Combine the Augeo, fragrance oil and diffuser dye in the measuring cup, stirring thoroughly. Pour the mixture into the diffuser bottle using the funnel.

2. Screw the cap on, and shake the bottle to mix. Tip the bottle at an angle (without spilling the contents), so some of the mixture comes into contact with the cork/wood inlay cap.

3. The scent will gradually release via the cap, and is detectable within an hour if placed into a small space such as car or locker. Tip the bottle so more of the mixture goes into the cork/wood whenever the scent deteriorates.

4. Keep all filled diffusers upright to avoid spillages, and away from direct sunlight and sources of ignition.

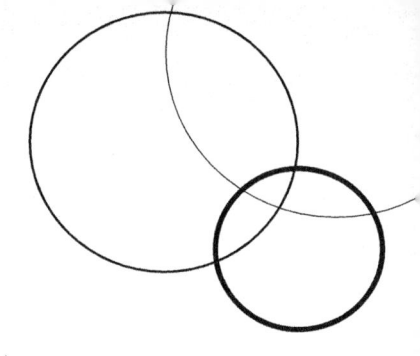

Part 4:

Legislation

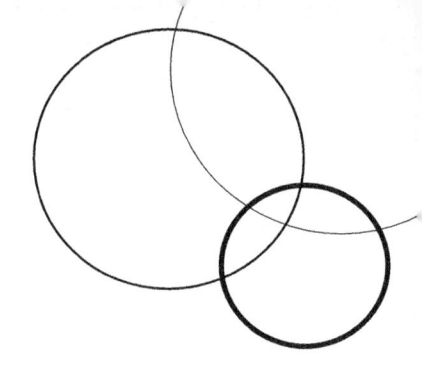

Part 4: Legislation

4.1 Legislation

This part takes you through the legislation that is relevant to wax- melt makers and sellers. It looks at the following:
- CLP (European Regulations) 2008
- Food Imitation Regulations 1989
- Intellectual Property
- Consumer Rights Act 2015
- Consumer Contract Regulations 2013

It is important to research each aspect thoroughly to gain a better understanding. Reading through this Part is a start, as is visiting the included links. You may also wish to consult with a qualified professional.

Failure to comply with the various pieces of legislation may result in one or more of the following:
- Receiving a cease-and-desist letter
- Having to pay a fine

- Having to pay for legal proceedings
- Prosecution
- Your business being forced to close

It is therefore important to ensure that the products you make and the branding you use are legally compliant.

4.2 CLP

Since 2009, this seemingly innocent combination of three letters has become the trigger for mild anxiety and general loathing amongst the wax-melt making community. Heavy sighing could be heard across the land as makers searched online for sticker templates, all the while contemplating a move to a warmer country, well outside the EU.

So what does CLP stand for and why is it so important?

CLP stands for **Classification, Labelling and Packaging**. Its formal name is "European Regulation (EC) No 1272/2008 on Classification, Labelling and Packaging (CLP)."

As its full name indicates, CLP is part of legislation decided by the European Union, of which the UK was a Member State at the time of its introduction. The UK was therefore legally obliged to implement CLP, so the regulations were transposed into – and are therefore now part of – UK law. Brexit does not affect the CLP requirements for the UK, so the regulations are retained – with some minor changes – in UK law via The Chemicals (Health and Safety) and Genetically Modified Organisms (Contained Use) (Amendment etc.) (EU Exit) Regulations 2020 (also known as the UK Statutory Instrument 2020 Number 1567).

The objective of CLP is to protect the health of humans and

the environment. A CLP (or hazard) label informs all users about any hazardous substances – and any mixtures containing those substances – with various warnings and statements.

Take a look at your bottle of disinfectant, for example. On the back of the bottle will be a CLP/hazard label comprised of various signal words, hazard statements and precautionary statements. The signal word states "Danger" or "Warning". The hazard statements state that the mixture "causes serious eye irritation", and is also "harmful to aquatic life". The precautionary statements tell you to therefore "wear eye protection" and "avoid release to the environment". In effect, the CLP label on your disinfectant is telling you not to pour the mixture onto your eyeballs or into a nearby river, because to do so will harm both you and the environment.

4.3 How does CLP apply to wax melt makers?

Wax melts are a mixture of wax and fragrance (or essential) oils. It is these oils that are considered to be hazardous in the wax melt mixture, so any wax melts you sell or otherwise distribute must be classified, labelled and packaged accordingly.

CLP does not just apply to wax melts. It applies to all home fragrance products that contain fragrance such as candles and diffusers.

4.4 How does CLP work practically?

First is the **classification**. The toxicological data of a substance or mixture is used to determine whether or not that substance or mixture meets the hazard classification criteria. The hazards are then assigned a hazard class and a category. The hazard classes cover physical and health hazards, as well as those affecting the environment, and any other hazards.

Next is the **labelling**. Think of the users in this part of the process as any of the fragrance oil suppliers listed in this book, who communicate the hazards 'downstream' to you. The fragrance oil suppliers do this via the labelling on bottles of fragrance oils and the supply of Safety Data Sheets (as explained in Part 1) on their websites.

As a maker in receipt of this labelling and the Safety Data Sheets, you are next in the supply chain to be alerted to any hazards in the fragrance oil you are using and how best to manage any risks associated with those hazards.

When you use a fragrance oil to make your wax melts, the original hazards labelled on that oil will change and it becomes your responsibility to inform the end user of these new hazards in the wax melt mixture. And that end user is your customer.

So how do you find out the new hazards in order to inform your customers? Your fragrance oil supplier will tell you. Suppliers usually provide makers with the CLP information at the 10% fragrance oil ratio free of charge, so you can simply copy and paste the information onto your labels and attach them to your wax-melt packaging. Should you use more than 10% fragrance oil in your melts, however, a different label is required (since the change in percentage has changed the applicable hazards).

Example

Let's say you have ordered a Mint fragrance oil to use in wax melts. The SDS for Mint is on the supplier's website, so you have a look through it. Section 2 of the SDS lists the hazards that apply to Mint at its 100% concentration, that is, in its undiluted-with-other-substances state. Section 8 of the SDS lists the precautions that apply to these hazards. The supplier is also obliged to communicate these hazards and precautions to you via the label on the bottle.

Once you receive the Mint fragrance oil you read the label on the bottle. One hazard statement tells you that it may cause an allergic skin reaction. The precautionary statement advises you, therefore, to wear protective gloves and to wash your hands and skin thoroughly after handling. You take the advised precautions and make wax melts using Mint, measuring out 10g of the oil and combining it with 100g of melted wax. Now that you have combined the fragrance oil with the wax, the 100% concentration of the fragrance oil has decreased in the mixture. The mixture is now composed of 10% fragrance oil and 90% wax. This change in oil percentage has changed the hazards and therefore changed the required pictograms and statements.

You visit the supplier's website and they have provided a label template for Mint when used at the 10% fragrance oil load. You use this information to create your CLP label and attach it to your wax-melt packaging.

4.5 Labelling elements

Regardless of size, CLP applies! (How is that for a handy rhyme?)

Pictograms and statements must be displayed in a certain way on hazardous substances and mixtures.

The label must be at least 52mm x 74mm in size and attached to the product so that it can be seen prior to purchase and before use. Most makers – if not all – attach their CLP labels to the back of the wax melt packaging.

It is also becoming increasingly common for makers who sell online to incorporate the CLP information into their product descriptions.

For products of 125ml and over, your CLP label must have the following:

1. **Product identifier**: The name of your product

2. **Pictogram(s)**: these visual warnings correspond to the hazard statements and alert users to the presence of hazardous chemicals. They are diamond-shaped with a red border and a white background and measure at least 1cm square

3. **Signal words**: Words such as "Warning", or "Danger", depending on which of these is triggered

4. **EH208 information**: relates to allergens triggered by any hazards. Depending on the nature and severity of the hazards there is a maximum number of allergens that can be included on the CLP label

5. **Hazard** or **H statements**: Used in conjunction with the pictograms, these inform the customer of the hazards present in your product, e.g. "H317 – May cause an allergic skin reaction"

6. **Precautionary** or **P statements**: Corresponding to each hazard statement, these advise the customer of what to do in order to avoid or minimise the hazards in the product, e.g. "P280 – wear eye protection"

7. **Supplier identification**: Your information, including your business name, registered address and contact telephone number.

For products below 125ml, your label must have the following:
- Product identifier
- Signal words
- EH208 information
- Supplier identification

And EITHER the:
- Pictogram (s)

OR the
- Hazard statements and
- Precautionary statements

4.6 Can I use the same pictograms and statements on every label?

No. Every fragrance oil is different, triggering its own set of hazards. So for every fragrance oil you use, there is different information on the label.

4.7 So which pictograms and statements do I use?

Your supplier will tell you. Whenever you buy a fragrance oil, the supplier is obliged to inform you of the hazards that apply at both 100% concentration (this is for your information) and at the smaller concentrations which are usually of 10% and 25% (this is for your customers information). You simply copy and paste the applicable pictograms and statements onto your labels and edit any other fields as necessary.

4.8 Are there any cases in which I do not need a CLP label?

No. CLP will always apply to home fragrance products that use fragrance or essential oils, because they are mixtures of potentially hazardous substances.

Not all fragrance oils contain *allergens*, however, so the pictogram, signal words and EH208 information will not be included on the label if this is the case. The following wording should be added instead:

"This substance contains no known allergens in accordance with European Regulation (EC) No 1272/2008"

Further reading:

The Health & Safety Executive (HSE) website provides a summary of CLP: https://www.hse.gov.uk/chemical-classification/legal/clp-regulation.htm

The HSE also provides guidance on CLP and the various hazard pictograms: http://www.hse.gov.uk/chemical-classification/labelling-packaging/hazard-symbols-hazard-pictograms.htm

For a full list of hazard statements, visit: https://www.msds-europe.com/h-statements/

Read more about the enforcement of CLP labelling: https://www.hse.gov.uk/chemical-classification/legal/enforcement-clp-regulation.htm

Things to think about:

What does CLP mean for your wax-melt business? Consider time and expenses.

How many suppliers have you used that provide the required SDS and CLP information? And how easily accessible is this information on their websites?

4.9 Other labelling

In addition to CLP labelling, there is other information that you may wish to include with your products.

Having this additional information does not make you immune to other laws, however, so you will still need to ensure that your products are compliant in other ways.

"Keep out of reach of children and pets"

Some CLP information already includes this statement. Wax melts are often brightly coloured or kept in brightly coloured packaging, so are very tempting to children who may play with or consume the melts.

There is also a risk of injury to pets. Like children, pets are very inquisitive and may sniff or touch the melt while it is in use. Some pets are also extremely sensitive to scents.

"Do not eat"

Wax melts come in a variety of scents and shapes and I often see makers selling melts in packaging meant for chocolates and sweets like advent calendars. Having a "Do not eat" statement may provide some sort of warning (but not legal protection. The Food Imitation regulations are covered in the next section).

"Do not leave wax melts unattended while in use"

Similar to candle safety labelling, this advice can also be included on your wax-melt labelling. From a practical perspective, people rarely sit with their wax melt the whole time it is melting, but this advice may prompt them to monitor it regularly for liquid wax overflow and any other unsafe occurrences.

"How to use wax melts"

You may want to include some general directions on how to use wax melts. Some wax-melt makers put a little card in with their products, others put it on labels attached to packaging.

4.10 Food Imitation Regulations 1989

The Food Imitations (Safety) Regulations 1989 prohibit any products that look like or imitate food, when those products are not actually food.

Such products are considered potentially dangerous because they may cause injury or other health risk if eaten by someone who believes the product to be food.

The regulations prohibit the following (emphasis added):

- the *marketing,*

- *import,* and
- *manufacture* of

products that look like foodstuffs but that are not in fact edible.

The regulations prohibit the supply of goods that have **one or more** of the following features:
- form
- odour
- colour
- appearance
- packaging
- labelling
- volume

that people, particularly children, could confuse with food.

If there is a risk of people and children putting the product in their mouth, sucking or swallowing, which may cause death or injury, then that product is prohibited. 'Injury' is defined as including choking, strangulation, cutting, poisoning, or causing a child to vomit.

Let's say you want to make a wax melt using a cupcake-shaped mould you bought from a catering shop (this particular feature of the melt will come under *form*). You want to scent it with a chocolate muffin fragrance oil (*odour*), sprinkle the top of the melt with sugar decorations (*appearance*), place it in a cupcake box (*packaging*), and call it a "Cupcake scented Wax Melt" (*labelling*). By having one or more of the features (as indicated in italics), the cupcake wax melt becomes subject to the regulations, which makes it prohibited under UK law.

Do not forget that having even just **one** feature in your

melts triggers the regulations. For example, wax melts of a certain size (*form*) or that look like fudge or chocolate bars (*appearance*) are subject to the regulations. Always check with your Trading Standards office before you make melts that could potentially imitate food. It is not worth the risk.

Further reading:

An excellent summary of the regulations and further examples: https://www.businesscompanion.info/en/quick-guides/product-safety/food-imitations

Things to think about:

Are you planning to make any melts that are subject to the Food Imitation Regulations? If so, what can you do to mitigate this?

4.11 Intellectual Property

It would take a whole book to cover intellectual property, however it is worth mentioning – albeit briefly – here.

Intellectual property concerns the ownership – and the protection of that ownership – over anything 'unique' that is created by someone.

UK intellectual property (IP) law is split into four types: designs, trademarks, patents and copyright. The type that applies will depend on the product, idea, or work created.

Under the right intellectual property type, you may be able to protect the following:

- your business name (trademark)
- your business logo (trademark)
- the styles or designs of your wax melts (design)
- the names of your wax melts (trademark)

With some exceptions, this protection is not free or automatically conferred, so in most cases you will need to apply and pay for it.

Once you have protection others cannot imitate or take your intellectual property such as your business name or product names unless they want to deal with the legal consequences.

If you feel strongly about your business and the direction it is going, by all means, protect it. However, if you are making melts using the same moulds and fragrance oil suppliers as other melt makers, think about whether handing over money for a potentially arduous process is worth it.

Intellectual property works both ways.

Just as you can protect your wax-melt designs and business name from others, other businesses can protect themselves from you. Found some distinctive cartoon mouse-shaped moulds? Unfortunately you cannot sell wax melts explicitly naming that design; it belongs to another business. Making melts scented with a particular 'numbered' luxury fragrance? You cannot name – or refer in any way to – that particular perfume in your wax-melt's design, description or promotion.

Perhaps you are tempted to use the same font as a popular bath bomb brand to promote your *lush*-smelling melts?

Do not do it unless you have permission. Without permission, UK law considers this as profiting from the goodwill of another business, and it is this misrepresentation that has the potential to damage the other business. Known as 'passing off', it is another type of enforceable intellectual property.

If you do plan on using the intellectual property of another business, you can ask for their permission to use it (which will not be cheap or is even guaranteed).

Further reading:

https://www.gov.uk/intellectual-property-an-overview

https://www.gov.uk/using-somebody-elses-intellectual-property

Things to think about:

Do any of the melts you make infringe intellectual property rights?

How could you mitigate these infringements?

4.12 Consumer Rights Act 2015

The Consumer Rights Act 2015 essentially enables anyone who has bought products or services to be entitled to a refund or repair if that product or service meets any of the three criteria below, subject to how long the customer has had the product or services for.

Claims under the Act can only be made against the seller – and not the manufacturer – of the products, so if you make melts on a wholesale basis for others to sell in their shops, it is the seller of your melts who deals with the claim.

Quality, purpose and description

Under the Act the products you sell must be of satisfactory quality, fit for purpose and as described. If your products do not satisfy any of these three criteria, customers can make a claim under the Act.

The 30 day right to reject

Customers have a legal right to a full refund if products/services fail to meet any of the three criteria above, but only if they claim within thirty days from the date they took ownership of the product.

After 30 days: repair or replace

If it has been thirty one days or up to a period of six months since the customer took ownership of the product, the retailer is given the opportunity to repair or replace the product, before the customer can ask for a refund.

Customers can state their preference for a repair or replacement, but it is normally the retailer who decides and they usually choose the cheaper or easier option.

After 30 days: refund or reduction

Should repair or replacement be unsuccessful, customers can claim a refund or a price reduction if they wish to keep the product.

Customers are entitled to a full or partial refund instead of a repair or replacement in any of the following circumstances:

- the cost of the repair or replacement is disproportionate to the value of the product
- a repair or replacement is impossible
- a repair or replacement would cause the customer significant inconvenience
- the repair would take an unreasonably long amount of time.

It is helpful for both you and your customers to have a point of reference when it comes to these rights, so if you sell online, have them easily visible or accessible at point of sale.

The Act also details the following:

- The Six Month fault
- The Six Year claim
- Delivery rights

Further reading and consulting with a qualified professional is definitely advisable for this subject!

Further reading:

https://www.which.co.uk/consumer-rights/regulation/consumer-rights-act

4.13 Consumer Contracts Regulations 2013

The Consumer Contracts Regulations provide additional protection to consumers in terms of order cancellations and distance selling.

The onus is on businesses to provide certain information to customers at the point of sale and while the specific information varies depending on whether the product is sold online or face-to-face, at the very least a satisfactory description of the goods is required.

The Regulations cover the following:

- Right to cancel
- Delivery of goods
- Returning faulty goods

Visit the link below to gain a better understanding of the Regulations, and consult a qualified professional if necessary.

Further reading:

https://www.which.co.uk/consumer-rights/regulation/consumer-contracts-regulations

Things to think about:

Do you understand UK consumer rights well enough to ensure that you can accommodate them in your selling policies?

4.14 Trading Standards

Contrary to what you may have read on Facebook, Trading Standards are there to help you. My local Trading Standards office say they would always advise, rather than penalise, in the first instance. So if you have any questions or need advice about food imitation or the legalities of selling online, contact yours!

Frustratingly, the advice provided from one Trading Standards office may differ from another, particularly on CLP requirements. It is definitely worth bringing all of your CLP-related materials and any products in their finalised packaging with you to the appointments you have with a Trading Standards officer. It is advisable to keep hold of all correspondence you have had with your Trading Standards office.

Find your local Trading Standards Office: https://www.tradingstandards.uk/consumers/support-advice

4.15 Trading status

If you are new to selling, you may not want to register as a sole trader, especially if you do not plan to sell wax melts in the long term. You can therefore skip this process if you do not think it will apply to you. However, if you earn more than £1,000 from your wax melt business in a year, you are legally required to register.

Sole trading essentially means sole responsibility. You have full ownership and control over aspects including your business name and profits, but also are solely liable for all its debts and other responsibilities.

The UK government's website is an excellent introduction to setting up your business as a sole trader: https://www.gov.uk/set-up-sole-trader

Another way to trade is as a limited company. Trading as a limited company is different from sole trading, as you are legally "separate" from your business, legally and financially.

The UK government's website also provides information on setting up as a limited company: https://www.gov.uk/set-up-limited-company

4.16 Insurance

While not legally required, you can take out some form of insurance once you decide to sell your melts.

Insurance protects you and your business should anything untoward happen to a customer because they were using your products. You can also get insurance to cover your place of work.

Most craft fairs – the largescale ones in particular – require you to have public liability insurance in order to sell at their fairs.

See the Suppliers section for a recommended insurance service.

4.17 The importance of record keeping

It is advisable to get into the habit of documenting your supplies and processes. Even if you decide not to sell your melts, it is handy to have a record of how much you have invested – and tested – in the endeavour. If you register as a trader, you are required to submit tax returns and keep records of your business sales and expenses, so the sooner you start a record keeping system the better.

Batch records (covered in s4.19) will also come in very useful if you ever have customer complaints about the melts you make (s4.21).

4.18 Invoices and receipts

I keep both the electronic versions of all my invoices and receipts (super easy since everything is emailed these days), as well as the paper versions (not so easy when filing is not your forte).

4.19 Batch records

For ease of traceability, keep records of the batches you have made, and record the materials and suppliers that you used with each batch. You can use **Worksheet 3: Batch Record** for this.

It is a good idea to record a batch number on every melt you make and sell. You can do this by writing the batch number on one of the labels that you usually attach to your wax-melt packaging, or create separate batch number labels and attach those to the packaging.

Even if you do not end up selling, you will still have a record of the materials and processes you used for each melt you have made, which will come in handy for future reference.

4.20 Suppliers batch numbers

Suppliers usually provide a batch code for every item they send to you, which will usually be on the item itself, or on the invoice.

If you see no batch number listed and you need it, contact them and ask for it.

4.21 Providing good customer service

Think about how would you provide good customer service in the following situation:

A customer complains that the melts they bought from you have no hot throw. What do you do next?

1) Confirm that you are maker/seller of the products

It is the very first thing you should do. Ask the customer to confirm the order number, which will be on the email or paper receipt. If the product was purchased from an approved retailer, they will need to contact the retailer in the first instance.

Check through the details to make sure everything is in order.

You are not just confirming that the concern is legitimate, but also keeping a trail on your purchasing systems should you need to process a refund.

2) Take the customer's concerns seriously

It is always disappointing to buy something and not have it work the way it should. Every customer is a valued customer and if they are not impressed with how you handle their complaint they will go elsewhere and very likely tell others about their negative experience. Apologise for their experience and reassure them that you will find out what has happened.

3) Check your processes

Consult your batch records to confirm you followed all the usual processes for melting, pouring, adding fragrance oil, any dyes and curing.

4) Test the product yourself

If you have a melt from that batch available, check the hot throw. You can also ask others to test for you and get their feedback.

5) Check your supplies

Check the supplier's batch numbers for the materials you used to make the final product. In this case it would be the wax and the fragrance oil.

Contact the suppliers of these materials and explain what the customer has told you. If asked, provide confirmation of your order number and the batch numbers labelled on the wax and fragrance oils.

Let us assume you have followed these steps.

A few days later the supplier contacts you and says that they have received similar queries from other makers regarding that particular batch of wax. Apparently the batch was stored under unusually extreme temperature conditions at the manufacturing plant, so they are now contacting all customers who bought affected batches (you included) and offering replacements.

6) Follow up quickly and appropriately

Do not keep your customer waiting for long while you investigate. After testing and checking your batch records, follow up with the customer in good time. Check your refund and replacement policy and explain which options you can offer to them.

Even if you do not fully agree with their concerns, if it is their first time reporting an issue to you, give them the benefit of the doubt and offer to send a replacement free of charge, or a refund.

If they are known to regularly request refunds or replacements from you or other makers, however, you will need to be stricter and consider the financial impact that such a customer has on your business. In these circumstances it is prudent to ensure that your returns policy states the customer has to pay for postage if they are returning an item. You will usually find that once you ask such customers to provide proof of purchase and/or send back their item, that will be the last you will hear from them.

Things to think about:

Will you keep batch records of every melt you make even if the melts are just for personal use? Will you keep paper or electronic records?

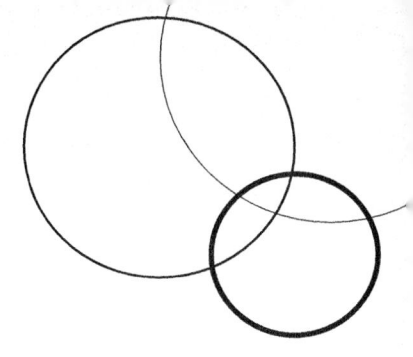

Part 5:

Build your brand

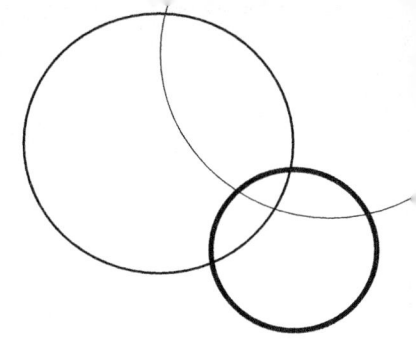

Part 5: Build your brand

5.1 Build your brand

Some wax-melt sellers possess a creative flair that is apparent in every melt they make. They know which trends to follow, which colours go well together and which pictures look great on their Instagram accounts.

If you feel lacking in this area, I assure you that there are ways in which you can find your own voice and build a brand you can be proud of. You do not need to be a graphic designer or the next Van Gogh to create a good brand!

There is a fair amount of work involved when creating a brand. Use **Worksheet 5: Brand Design** to kickstart your ideas and go from there!

5.2 Create a brand you love

It is important to be happy with the brand you are creating. If you do not like your logo or your colour scheme, for example, the lack of enthusiasm will become obvious to customers.

A genuine passion for your products will be evident in your photos, descriptions and customer service. So make sure that you are happy with all aspects of your brand design before you start selling.

5.3 Find your voice

To start, look at the little ways in which you are different from all the other makers out there. You may all use the same heart moulds and fragrance oils, but take a closer look at you and what you have to offer.

For example, where are you based? Do you live in the countryside, surrounded by rolling green hills and beautiful nature? You may consider it boring and quiet, but to potential customers living in busy cities, products made so close to nature are very appealing. You can make this part of your brand!

You can carry this theme through to the content you put on your social media feeds and website. Share pictures of your local lavender fields and orchards; even out of your kitchen window if the view is particularly lovely!

Maintain the theme with the wax melts you make. How about making lavender-scented wax melts and decorating them with the lavender you freshly pick every day? Do you live near a beekeeper? How about using some of their beeswax in your melts?

All of these factors are your *influences*. Make them part of your business idea and you have got your *brand*!

5.4 Refine your brand

Once you have identified your influences, work on refining

and clarifying them so you have a brand that is recognizable to customers.

Let's go with the living-in-the-countryside example. You have decided to use freshly-picked lavender flowers to decorate your melts, so how about making this a permanent feature of your brand?

You can carry the lavender aspect through to your brand name, brand logo, even brand tagline.

Here are some ideas I came up with:

Lavender Cottage

Cottage logo

Wax melts homemade in the English countryside

Nature's Dream

Lavender logo

Making nature part of your home

The Lil Lavender Ladybird

Ladybird logo

Cute and fragrant wax melts

These are just initial ideas. As mentioned earlier, you will need to think about things thoroughly in order to come up with a brand that you are completely happy with. And do not forget to check that the brand name you want to use is not already taken by another business.

5.5 Other branding aspects to consider

Fonts and colour schemes are also important when informing a potential customer about your brand. A customer can perceive your brand's personality with just one glance at these characteristics and using them will help a customer to decide whether or not they want to find out more about your products.

Fonts

Romantic and cursive fonts are normally used by countryside and feminine-inspired brands, while the minimalist and bold fonts are used to great effect by metropolitan brands such as MAC and NARS.

Quirky fonts emphasise the 'unique and boutique' aspects of a brand; Diptyque is a wonderful example of this.

What does your font say about your brand?

Colour scheme

Your products could come in all colours of the rainbow and you may want things such as your packaging and logo to reflect that. Alternatively, you may want the products to speak for themselves, so choose packaging that will not detract from them. Lush is a good example of this: their plain black pots, combined with a (now internationally recognised) bold font, showcase the vivid colours of their huge product range.

Alternatively you may want a chic and restrained palette, such as pinks and greys for a modern 'influencer' look.

How about the classic white and black? The White Company and Jo Malone are good examples of this simple luxury aesthetic. Their products sell in their millions to customers who use them to both scent and decorate their homes.

What does your colour scheme tell customers about your brand?

5.6 Getting help from professionals

If you are not confident with your artistic skills, you can hire a professional to design and draw your logo. An online search will bring up hundreds of suggestions, as will putting a query up in a couple of Facebook wax-melt groups; plenty of makers are happy to recommend a designer that they themselves have used. This, however, is another expense.

I believe that hiring people to help you with aspects of your business where you lack expertise is worth considering and frees you up to concentrate on other things.

5.7 Establish your brand

You have identified and refined your brand. Now you have to establish it, and that means getting your brand out there!

Whether you are selling in person or online, promoting your brand will garner interest which will ultimately lead to sales.

There are plenty of books and helpful articles online that cover this subject in more depth but here are my tips to get you started.

5.8 Product packaging

Your logo and brand name should be visible on your products, not just to identify your product to the customer but as a promotional tool. When others see who made their friend's products, they will be tempted to buy them too.

Have your logo and business name printed on labels to attach to your packaging. Some makers have labels made for each individual scent. If you own a decent colour printer and source some blank labels, you can print your own, otherwise go to the Suppliers section for recommended printing services.

Consider carrying your branding through to the other packaging that is handled by the customer. The tissue paper used to wrap the melts, even the packing tape you use to package customer orders can all be customised with your brand. These aspects of a purchase are also important in a time when customers like to film "unboxing" videos.

5.9 Purchase extras

I would always include wax melt samples with customer orders, as I found that nine times out of ten the customer would purchase the full- size version the next time they ordered.

I also included a business card and a brochure, so customers had a visual point of reference. Never underestimate the value of printed materials when it comes to getting more sales! Avon is an excellent example. As well as selling online, they distribute catalogues with "scratch and sniff" sections amongst the pages.

You can also include promotional items such as stickers and cards with discount codes or Instagram prompts ("tag your purchase"). Customers generally love receiving extras, so take advantage of that and promote, promote, promote!

5.10 Social media

Social media is such a huge part of our lives and everyday millions of people share their photos and updates on social media such as Facebook and Instagram.

Instagram is a very useful promotional tool. Start with a simple scroll through all the photos that use the hashtag #waxmelts or #waxmeltaddict and thousands of photos appear. These users are your potential customers!

Use these hashtags when posting your content, so other users can find you.

When you have a wax-melt account on Instagram, make sure to post your brand's beginnings, influences, even manufacturing processes. A photo of mica being stirred into liquid wax, for example, is very hypnotic.

You can also set up a Facebook page for your wax-melt business. Wax- melt sales and swaps are huge on Facebook; whenever I log on, a new wax-melt page/group appears. You can add a 'Shop Now' link to your page, promote your products to potential customers across Facebook for a small fee and easily respond to queries.

Some melt-makers set up Facebook groups for their businesses so they can easily adjust privacy settings for customers only, which adds a more 'VIP' feel. Experiment with both and see which you prefer.

5.11 Online selling platforms

There are number of online selling platforms where you can easily set up shop to sell your melts, including Ebay, Amazon and Etsy but they all vary in terms of commission and online presence.

Use **Worksheet 4: Website Comparison** to help you research and compare the various online selling options available.

5.12 Your own website

If you find selling through platforms like Etsy too restrictive in terms of personalisation and commission, having your own website is a very appealing alternative.

When you have your own website you have control over how it looks and how much you earn. You will also have an exclusive domain name, which gives a more professional feel to your brand.

However you sell your melts online, make sure to use good photos, clear descriptions and competitive prices. Clarify postage fees, dispatch and delivery, refunds and exchanges. These can form part of the FAQ or Terms and Conditions sections of your website, or the product descriptions.

Setting up your own website takes time. If you would rather concentrate on other aspects of your business, consider paying a professional to set up the website for you. Make sure to provide a comprehensive brief detailing exactly how you want your site to look, and include any images as inspiration to provide the designer with a good starting point.

Worksheet 6: Pre-launch Checklist will help you prepare for your business launch day.

5.13 Events and exhibitions

Who doesn't love a good fair? Having a stall at events like fairs and exhibitions is an effective way to promote your brand, especially if it is in time for celebrations such as Christmas and Valentine's Day.

Visit some events beforehand as part of your preparation. Observe footfall, stall set-ups, premium stall locations, popular payment methods and how customers work their way through the event.

Look at how sellers attract custom at these events. And is there local or nationwide advertising? And also consider the stall fee, as at big events this could cost thousands.

Check what'll you need to take with you, such as:

- Your own table and other stall/stand equipment
- Table coverings
- Displays such as baskets or shelving
- Ways to advertise your business and inform of prices
- Sustenance to get you through the day
- Accepted payment methods, e.g. card reader, or cash only and receipts
- Amount of stock to bring (depending on estimated visitor numbers)
- Public liability insurance
- Deals you could have, that are exclusive to the event
- Promotional materials to hand out, e.g. leaflets, samples
- Any demonstrations you could do to entice customers
- Bags to pack purchases

5.14 Maintaining your presence

Once you become an established seller, you will be able to identify your regular customers and your most popular scents.

Stay consistent and keep selling what your customers buy. It sounds obvious, but some makers get bored and change their products – in addition to their branding – without thinking about their loyal customers.

If you do feel bored with some of your products, consider adding different products to your range. Part 6 goes through ways in which you can expand your business.

5.15 Customer feedback

Ask your customers what they would like to see next. Do they want more formats, weird scents, or bundle deals? A common mistake made by businesses is overlooking what their customers want. When given the opportunity, customers can be a great source of inspiration!

Create a poll on your social media channels to get feedback and ideas.

5.16 Keeping up with trends

It is important to keep up with wax-melt trends, especially around seasonal times such as Christmas and Valentine's Day.

At Christmas 2019, christmas-tree-shaped clamshells were incredibly popular, while at Christmas 2020, gonks (Scandanavian gnomes) were everywhere!

People tend to gravitate towards cosy scents in the colder months and the lighter scents when it starts to warm up. Think about the ways in which you could match your melts to this trend.

5.17 Promotions

Engage with existing and potential customers via promotions.

Many sellers host giveaways in return for customers tagging friends on Instagram, or include scratch cards with every order to give customers a chance to win more of their products.

I like the idea of asking customers to "name the melt", as it really encourages everyone to get involved. Customers have great fun in coming up with unique - and often hilarious — names for melts and will definitely buy a product that they helped create.

5.18 Wax-melt challenges

I used to create wax-melt challenges on Instagram, and these were such a fun way to engage both customers and non-customers. I am smiling now just thinking about it!

Wax melt challenges are when you use a different melt each day for a whole month (or other defined period) and share what you have melted on Instagram using hashtags so everyone else participating can see.

Your choice that day will be whatever the seller has put on the 'challenge calendar'. Monday's challenge, for example, can be to "melt a blue wax melt", while Tuesday's challenge will be to "melt a wax melt that reminds you of your ex". See, they are fun!

5.19 Wax-melt parties

Hosting wax-melt parties is another way to showcase your brand.

If you remember Tupperware parties, wax-melt parties work the same way. You can either have a brand representative (see below) to host or do it yourself.

Organise a date and time (evenings and weekends work well for most), a location, and work out how much stock to bring and how you would set it up. Have drinks and nibbles available, create a couple of party-exclusive deals and even some games if you think they would get the guests buying.

As with any kind of promotion, you need to consider the expenses that these kinds of events incur.

5.20 Brand representatives

Brand representatives can expand your brand to areas of the country that you may be otherwise unable to reach.

A lot of sellers choose loyal customers as brand representatives, others run competitions. However you recruit them, make sure you clarify what is expected of them and what benefits they will receive.

The brand representative model varies greatly amongst wax-melt sellers. Some representatives exclusively promote products on social media and provide customers with exclusive discount codes, others host wax melt parties and sell at events such as fairs. I have also seen brand representatives who actually make the wax melts themselves, and then attach the seller's brand labelling to the final product.

5.21 Collaborations

It is pretty much a given that once you start selling wax melts, you will receive a lot of messages from "influencers" who want to "collaborate"! When I was a seller I ignored all of them. Why? Because true influencers do not need to ask to collaborate; brands come to them and not the other way round. The people who send out scrappily or cringeworthy written 'media kit emails' are often just after free products in return for 'exposure'.

I have received some (unintentionally) hilarious messages

from self-proclaimed influencers. One was from a woman with ten Instagram followers, and whose pictures consisted of selfies shot under the cover of darkness. Her message read: "I love your melts! I am an influencer and would love to promote your melts. I can send you my ibdor". What is 'ibdor'? Answers on a postcard, please.

If you really can't resist the call of an influencer, offer to create a discount code for them to promote on their social media. This is the safest way for you to determine how serious they really are. If they refuse, well, there you have it.

In my opinion, collaborating with self-proclaimed influencers is not the best way for small businesses to earn money or gain exposure, especially if just starting out. You are better off paying to run adverts on Instagram and Facebook.

5.22 Donating to charities

As well as the influencer emails, I was contacted by people working for charities that were desperately in need of donations to their raffle or some other event.

In 2015 a woman claiming to be working on behalf of a charity contacted me via Etsy, asking for wax melt donations to a raffle. I felt guilty about the little boy she told me about, who had died a couple of years earlier and loved anything to do with the themed melts I had recently listed in my Etsy shop. I asked her to verify the charity, to which she sent me a link to a Facebook page. In my naivety I sent £50 worth of bubble-wrapped stock to the address provided on the Facebook page and waited. And waited. A couple of weeks after the raffle was due to take place I emailed her. Her reply: "We could not use any of your melts because they were all damaged". That was it. No hello or thank you, no apologies for delays in contacting me, not even a 'Best wishes'.

Some months later I mentioned what had happened to a fellow wax-melt maker. She told me someone from the same charity had also contacted her and she had sent them a generous amount of stock. When she contacted them to get an idea of how much her products had raised in the raffle, they told her that her melts were unusable and damaged. She had sent one hundred deli pot melts, all beautifully decorated with glitter and ornate embeds.

I thereafter swore off engaging with charities, legitimate or not. I doubt that these people know how much public trust is damaged with this type of behaviour, scam or not.

The lesson here is if you really want to help charitable causes, you can raise awareness and money yourself. Why not create a wax melt dedicated to a particular charity and donate the profits made or create a group event that you and your customers can participate in?

Things to think about:

How would you obtain customer feedback? Think about what questions to ask, doing a poll, etc.

What resources could you use to stay informed about trends in wax-melt making?

What promotions could you run to generate interest in your business?

What promotions could you run to generate sales of your products?

If you were to use brand representatives, what benefits would you offer them?

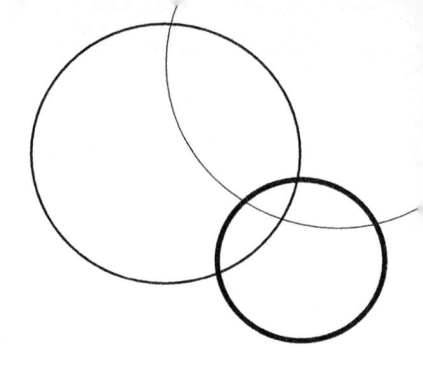

Part 6:

Expansion

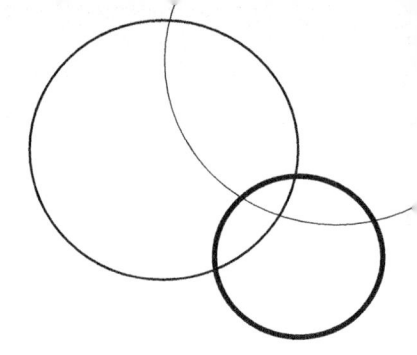

Part 6: Expansion

6.1 Expanding your range

You have tried all the techniques for making a variety of wax melts, found your favourite oils and a loyal customer base. Congratulations - you have established yourself as a successful wax-melt maker!

So what's next? How about adding more home fragrance goodies to your repertoire? This part of the book goes through the various ways in which you can expand your range and build on your brand.

Candles are an obvious add-on for a wax-melt business. They do, however, require a bigger investment compared with wax melts, both financially and testing-wise. And a separate book! Thus we will be focusing on the other types of add-ons here.

6.2 Add-ons

When you introduce further products into your business that serve the same purpose (i.e., scent) but differ in some way (i.e., by scenting the room using a different method, scenting clothes or scenting the skin), you are introducing "add-ons".

Typical add-on products for wax-melt makers include candles, scented sachets, simmering granules, diffusers and room sprays.

Add-ons are an effective way to keep your brand fresh, helping you retain existing customers as well as attract new ones. You will find that as you add on more products to your range, customers will tend to buy most – if not all – of their home fragrance products from you.

Start with a small number of fragrances for add-on products, selecting both the most popular scents that you sell in your wax melts and newer, more relevant scents i.e., the clean smelling, laundry-type fragrance oils for scented sachets.

6.3 Scented sachets

Scented sachets work in the same way as air fresheners and scented drawer liners: they can be hung or tucked in next to the item that the customer wants to scent. They are placed next to linen or clothing, in places like a laundry cabinet or wardrobe. They can also be hung in small spaces such as the car, lockers or even on coat hooks.

6.4 Wax tablets

Wax tablets are used in the same way as scented sachets and, provided no large decorations have been used, they can also be melted in a wax- melt burner. I prefer to hang them, as they look very pretty in spaces that would otherwise be empty.

Just be sure that you do not use wax tablets in environments where they are likely to melt and cause damage.

Project 10 in Part 3 shows you how to make hanging wax tablets that use orange slices as a natural decoration. Have a go!

6.5 Simmering granules

Simmering granules are small natural salt crystals or chunks that can be warmed like wax melts in a burner, or left as they are ('cold') to scent a room. I generally find their cold throw very weak compared with hot, but if you colour them in a vibrant shade and display a substantial amount of them in a huge glass vase for example, their visual impact alone can be stunning.

Some makers use dishwasher salts to make simmering granules, others use natural salt chunks. It is up to you which material you use.

Project 11 in Part 3 teaches you how to make simmering granules.

I find the name 'simmering granules' a tad redundant when the bigger salt crystals and chunks are used, so perhaps call yours something more descriptive like "scented salts" or "scented crystals".

6.6 Room sprays

Room sprays are profitable add-ons but it is vital to find a good formula that lasts in a room and does not leave a greasy residue on surfaces. Most fragrance oils can be used to make room sprays, although you will need to test them out with various room-spray bases, such as Augeo and perfumers' alcohol.

6.7 Diffusers

There are three types of diffuser; reed (which is the one most people are familiar with), hanging and electric.

Because of their compact size, hanging diffusers are a popular add-on for many wax-melt makers. They require a stable place to stand or hang from, so their fragrance can gradually diffuse through the diffuser cap and into the air. You should be able to smell their scent within an hour.

Project 12 in Part 3 teaches you how to make mini hanging diffusers.

6.8 Burners

Burners are easily profitable add-ons because people buying melts will usually need a burner with which to use those melts. Consider doing a 'bundle' or 'deal' which includes both a wax-melt burner and a selection of melts; these are very popular as gifts.

Always check that the burners you buy are suitable for use with wax melts. Check the burner label/description and, if you are still not sure, ask the supplier to confirm.

6.9 Bath and body products

Bath and body products are a fun add-on to wax-melt businesses, especially if the fragrances match those you already have in wax melts.

Soap bars, whipped shower fluffs, bubbly bath bars and fizzy bath bombs all have an allure of their own and make great gifts. You have a huge advantage over other wax-melt sellers if you know how to make them yourself!

Bath and body products are subject to a whole other set of regulations, however, so if you have the desire and finances to take up this venture, go for it!

For those of you who are not so inclined, why not approach other small businesses and get quotes for wholesale? A lot of bath and body product makers are happy to supply their products as 'white label', meaning you can use your own labels on their products, although the maker's business name and contact details are legally required to be included on the product label.

There are also a number of UK businesses that supply wholesale items such as candles and bath and body products. See the Suppliers section for some recommendations. Wholesale items are sold in bulk quantities so are a bigger investment; expect to spend at least £100 when you order.

Case Study: The Hertford Candle Co

www.thehertfordcandleco.com

Danielle Small owns The Hertford Candle Co, a home-fragrance business that developed organically from a career in home décor.

Her passion for creating home-fragrance products combined with a keen eye for luxurious accents has been key to building a truly stunning brand. In addition to candles and wax melts, The Hertford Candle Co also offers products including room sprays, fragrance lamps and body lotions. Danielle has the following advice for makers interested in expanding their product range:

"Make sure to develop and maintain good relationships with your customers, as they are usually the driving force for

deciding on new scents and add-on products for your range.

I also look at the latest trends and product releases to get an idea of what products will sell well for me in the future. Research is key if you want to be ahead of other wax-melt businesses, as is self-belief. Always stay true to yourself and your business."

6.10 Other products

As well as add-ons, you can use other products to broaden your range. By selling products related to your brand – but which are not home fragrance – you appeal to a wider customer base.

Let's say you own "Bee Scented", a business that makes and sells wax melts using a beeswax blend. Your logo is a big yellow and black bee. You decide to expand your product range by selling other bee-themed products such as keyrings, wallets and umbrellas, as these will appeal to the nature lovers – a sizeable demographic within the UK, which also includes gardeners and florists. You also decide to stock bath and body add-ons from another small business which includes hand creams and lip balms made with beeswax from local beekeepers.

Things to think about:

Which add-ons are a viable option for your business?

How many add-ons will you start with?

If you are buying add-ons or 'white-label' products, how will you cover yourself and your business in the event things go wrong? Consider non-delivery, broken or faulty products.

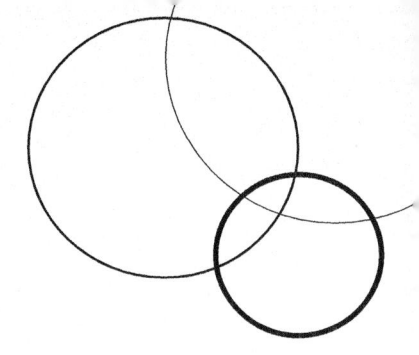

Worksheets

These worksheets may be reproduced and amended for personal use only.

Worksheet 1: Supplies List

Materials	Supplier	Cost

Total:

Equipment	Supplier	Cost

Total:

Worksheet 2: Wax Testing Record

Date made: _____
Test date: _____

Wax used: _____
Supplier: _____

Cost: £ _____ per kg   £ _____ per 5 kg
       £ _____ per 10 kg   £ _____ per 20 kg

Wax type:
Paraffin ☐   Plant-based ☐   Combination ☐

Wax format:
Block ☐   Flake ☐   Pellet ☐

Suitable for:
Clamshells ☐   Deli pots ☐   Silicone moulds ☐
Scoopable wax ☐   Squeezable wax ☐   Wax Brittle ☐

Maximum fragrance load: _____ %   Load used: _____ %

Suitable with dyes: Yes ☐   No ☐   N/A ☐

Melt temp: _____ degrees C/F
Pour temp: _____ degrees C/F
Add oils at temp: _____ degrees C/F
Cure time: _____ days/weeks

Notes/observations

Worksheet 3: Batch Record

Product: _____

Date made: _____
Test date: _____

Quantity: _____
FO load: _____ %

Format:

Clamshells ☐   Deli pots ☐   Silicone moulds ☐
Scoopable wax ☐   Squeezable wax ☐   Wax Brittle ☐

Supplies

	Name	Supplier	Batch no.
Wax			
Fragrance oil			
Dyes			
Decorations			

Temperature control

	degrees C/F
Melt	
Pour	
Cool	

Notes/observations

THE WAX MELT WORKBOOK   ZOE GEORGE

Worksheet 4: Website Comparison

Website/online marketplace name:
_____

Commission taken for each item sold:
Yes ☐ % per item: _____
None ☐

Cost of website per month: £ _____   N/A ☐

Maximum number of items I can list:

Main benefits:

Any disadvantages/restrictions:

Notes

Worksheet 5: Brand Design

Think about the following when designing and naming your brand and its products:

Starting a brand

- Styles and influences

- Ideal customer

- Wants to be known for... (provide a short summary as if you were talking to a potential customer)

- Colour schemes and palettes

- Fonts

- Logo ideas

Brand design
- Natural and eco friendly
- Romantic, feminine
- Modern, minimalist
- Quirky, bold
- Edgy, alternative
- Classic
- Other

Worksheet 6: Pre-launch Checklist

Edit/check off as necessary:

- [ ] Ready-made products
- [ ] Insurance
- [ ] Product/package labels, usage instructions
- [ ] CLP labels
- [ ] Thank you notes/business cards/samples to include with orders
- [ ] Envelopes, bubble wrap, boxes, tapes for packaging
- [ ] Website/online listings ready
- [ ] Social media announcements ready
- [ ] Introductory deals
- [ ] Postal charges sorted (especially for multiple buys)

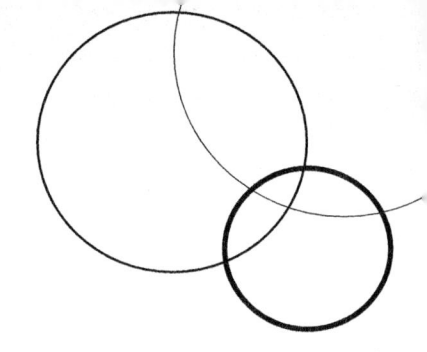

Troubleshooting

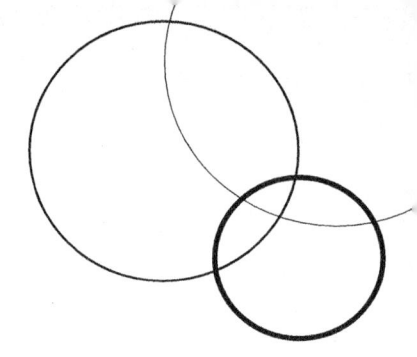

Troubleshooting

Problems are inevitable when trying something new and wax-melt making is no exception.

Below are the most common problems that occur when making wax melts and how to solve them.

Removing wax melts from moulds

If you are having trouble releasing melts from a mould, leave in a cool place (such as a fridge) for an hour or so beforehand. This will further harden the wax and slightly shrink it so it will slip out of the mould easily.

If your mould is of a delicate or fiddly design, slowly and carefully remove the melt by gently pushing through from the other side of the mould.

If this does not help, the problem may be that your wax is too soft (the result of too much fragrance oil, in which case you need to re-test and consider adding some stearin).

Frosting

Frosting is when cream-coloured speckles or 'frost' develops on the surface of the wax melt once it has hardened. Frosting is often the result of inconsistent temperature control during the making and curing stages.

To avoid frosting, ensure that you melt the wax to its

recommended temperature and have your fragrance oils and any dyes ready so you can combine and stir quickly. You may also need to adjust the temperature of the room you are making in; sudden temperature changes can contribute to frosting.

Some plant-based waxes are naturally prone to frosting, so the only way to get a wax that does not frost is by testing and getting feedback from other makers.

Not stirring in dyes properly can also result in 'colour frosting', where the colour looks uneven in the melt. Make sure to stir your dyes (whether they are liquid, block or mica powder) thoroughly in the liquid wax, distributing them thoroughly and check for any residue that may 'lump' together at the bottom of the container you are stirring in.

Lack of hot throw

This could be due to a number of factors, so finding the cause will be a process of elimination. Check the following:

- The wax has been cured for the recommended cure time

- You have used the optimum amount of fragrance oil

- Customer's melting methods: Electric burners do not burn as hot as tealight ones, so melts used with electric burners may not adequately melt to fully disperse their scent

- In rare instances, the wax and/or fragrance oils used are faulty. You will therefore need to check this with the supplier.

'Sinking' glitter

If you use glitter to decorate the surface of your melts in a silicone or plastic mould, sprinkle the mould with glitter before you pour the wax in.

Depending on which way the mould faces, you can also sprinkle glitter on the surface while the wax is still cooling but not while it is still hot (it will just sink and disappear) or once it has hardened, otherwise it will just slide off.

Dull looking melts

If your melts look dull when unmoulded, check your moulds! Sometimes the residue from all that making sticks in the corners of your mould, so a good scrub with dishwashing detergent and a stiff brush should sort it.

The wax could also be to blame. Plant-based waxes tend to vary from batch to batch, so you may find that the gloss you usually get on your melts is inconsistent or even non-existent.

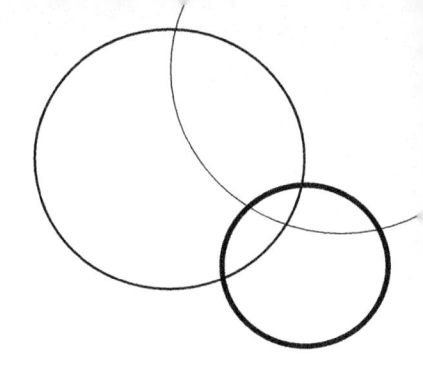

Suppliers and resources

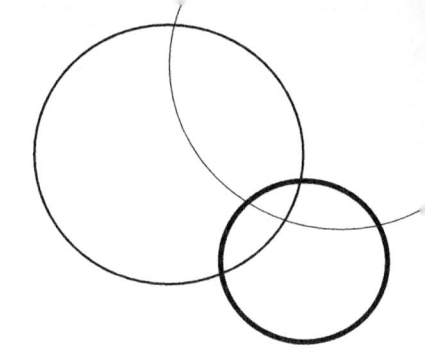

Suppliers and resources

Suppliers

Blossom Oils

Vickie supplies a lovely range of fragrance oils as well as waxes and clamshell packaging. Join her Facebook group to see her latest offers and popular scents.

www.blossomoils.co.uk

Candle Shack

Candle Shack is the UK's leading supplier of candle materials and equipment. Choose from a variety of waxes, dyes and fragrance and essential oils formulated specifically for use in home fragrancing products. Husband-and-wife owners Cheryl and Duncan also run the Candle Shack Community group on Facebook, which is an invaluable online resource for all candle and melt makers.

www.candle-shack.co.uk

Cello Express

Cello Express have cellophane bags in all shapes and sizes, so you are guaranteed to find packaging to suit your various wax-melt needs.

www.celloexpress.co.uk

Enchanted Oils

Enchanted Oils have an inspiring selection of fragrance oils in addition to perfumer's alcohol and mica. The owner, Donna, also runs a group on Facebook, where members can suggest new oils and other products.

www.enchantedoils.co.uk

Freshskin

Freshskin sell fragrance oils in all the popular scents, as well as dyes and waxes.

www.freshskin.co.uk

Globe Packaging

Globe Packaging supply bubble wrap, packaging tapes, boxes and padded envelopes.

www.globepackaging.co.uk

Kite Packaging

Kite Packaging have bubble wrap, boxes, padded envelopes and eco-friendly packing peanuts.

www.kitepackaging.co.uk

Livemoor

Livemoor sell all the essentials for wax-melt making, as well as supplies for soap making and flower crafts. I bought my very first bag of wax from here! Ah, memories...

www.livemoor.co.uk

NI Candle Supplies

NICS offer a range of fragrance oils, some not found anywhere else in the UK. Their website is super stylish and super addictive! Join their candle-making group on Facebook for advice on everything from fragrance loads to CLP.

www.nicandlesupplies.co.uk

Oasis Oils

Oasis Oils offers a wide range of fragrance oils, all strong and popular with customers. Louise also runs a group on Facebook for makers to show their wax melts and discuss upcoming oils.

www.oasisoils.co.uk

Randall's Candles

Randall's Candles have a huge range of supplies including dye chips, mini hanging diffusers and hundreds of fragrance oils.

www.randallscandles.co.uk

Sell The Smells

We UK-based makers can get hold of fragrance oils from Nature's Garden (a brand popular on the other side of the pond) from Sell The Smells. Expect to find some great fragrances here!

www.sellthesmells.co.uk

Shotfeet Emporium

Be tempted by their range of glitter shapes, super shimmer mica and silicone moulds.

www.shotfeet.com

Sparkle Town

Beautiful bio glitters and bio-glitter mixes, as well as lustrous micas in all colours of the rainbow.

www.sparkletown.co.uk

General Supplies can also be found at the following:
- eBay
- Amazon
- Lakeland

Wholesale

Ancient Wisdom

A giftware wholesaler, Ancient Wisdom sell ready-made candles, soaps, bath bombs and plant pots.

www.ancientwisdom.biz

Puckator

Another popular UK wholesaler, be tempted by floral print wallets, panda lip balms and sloth mugs as you browse the website.

www.puckator.co.uk

Services

Avery (Labels)

www.avery.co.uk

Ian Wallace Insurance

www.craftinsurance.co.uk

Vistaprint (Printed materials including labels and business cards)

www.vistaprint.co.uk

Resources

Keep up to date with things wax-melt and home fragrance -related on Instagram:

@thehomefragranceworkbooks

Get government advice about setting up a business:

https://www.gov.uk/set-up-business

If you are a supplier/service provider and would like to be featured on the book's social media, or in future editions of this book, please contact the author via email: itszoegeorge@gmail.com.

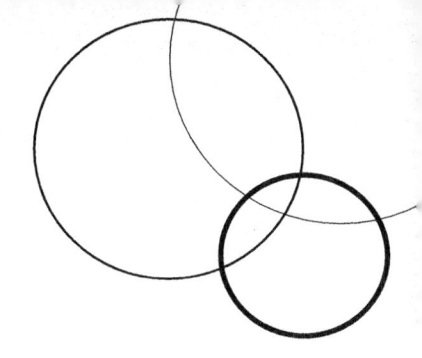

Interviews

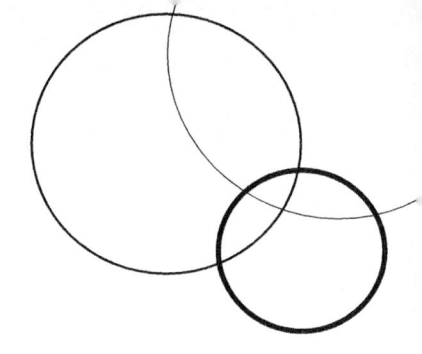

Interviews

When I first started writing The Wax Melt Workbook I knew that I wanted to interview suppliers. Supplying thousands of customers on a regular basis is no easy task and the two suppliers featured here are not just popular with makers but also lovely to boot. I hope you enjoy this rare insight into their worlds.

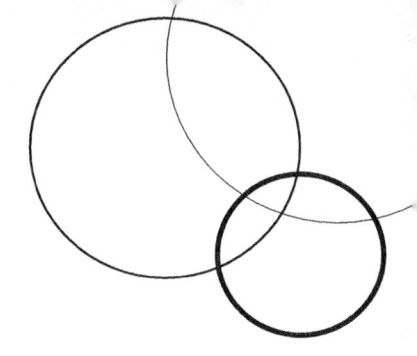

Interview with Louise Clark of Oasis Oils

Louise set up Oasis Oils in 2017 after becoming frustrated with the lack of certain fragrance oils for her own wax-melt business. She has since been supplying over 160 oils to satisfied customers all over the UK from her base in south Wales.

What is your favourite aspect of being a supplier?

I only buy in safe, top quality oils. I love that Oasis Oils helps makers create amazing products, which in turn helps to make their business successful.

And your least favourite aspect?

Social media is not something I have the time to focus on, but it is important for a business like mine. I therefore employ a fantastic IT 'chap' (as I like to call him!) who does my social media posts and maintains the Oasis Oils website. It takes a huge weight off my shoulders and gives me time to focus on the day-to-day running of Oasis Oils.

What is the most popular Oasis Oils fragrance oil?

It really depends on the time of year, although customers' year-round favourites are Eventus, Spring Awakening, Fairy

Laundry, Vanilla Lime and Black Opeum.

I do want to keep extending the Oasis Oils range, so keep your eyes peeled for future releases!

If you could improve one thing about how your run your business, what would it be?

All suppliers want to provide the absolute best service, but sometimes we do that to our own detriment, so I would like to improve my ability to 'switch off'. As I am sure a lot of self-employed people understand, it is all too easy to 'live' your business and forget about living your life. I need to stop checking my phone every evening and at the weekend, as it is important to relax and recharge. We work to live, not live to work.

What are you most proud of in your business?

I am extremely proud of Oasis Oils' reputation. My husband Andrew and I work very hard to provide top quality oils and excellent customer service. I feel our reputation and excellent reviews reflect that!

Quickfire questions

Where do you live?

I live in Cwmbran in South Wales with my husband Andrew, daughter Bethan and Luna, the dog princess!

Do you have a favourite scent?

My favourite perfume is Dior's Dolce Vita. It is all sorts of gorgeous; sherbet-like and sweet. Just beautiful.

If I had to pick just one fragrance from my oil range, it would be Vanilla Lime!

Do you have any hobbies?

I enjoy reading crime novels, watching Netflix and silliness. I love to laugh; life is too short to be too serious! Relaxing with a bottle of Mango Vodka in the garden with friends is another 'hobby' I enjoy.

Favourite place to be?

Anywhere with friends and family, especially if it is by the sea. I try to visit the coast as often as possible. We have a little caravan near the sea in Weston-super-Mare and we try to go there most weekends.

I also dream of travelling around all the beautiful countries in Europe, preferably on a cruise ship! It is so peaceful being out at sea, nothing as far as the eye can see except water. That is my idea of absolute bliss.

You can visit Louise's website at www.oasisoils.co.uk

Interview with Josie Boulter of Sparkle Town

Josie started Sparkle Town in 2019, with a passion for sourcing the most colourful glitters which had the least impact on the environment. Based in Letchworth Garden City, Hertfordshire, Sparkle Town supplies beautiful bio glitters in a variety of colours and mixes that are popular with all types of crafters.

What is your favourite aspect of being a supplier?

That I have played a part – however small – in the success of hundreds of wax-melt businesses. My customers often share pictures of their melts made using Sparkle Town products and I just love seeing the different ways in which my glitters and micas have been used.

And your least favourite aspect?

It can be difficult for me to switch off sometimes. I try to set aside time during the day just for me but I'm not very good at sticking to it!

What is the most popular Sparkle Town product?

The Unicorn Mix bio glitter, without a doubt!

Unicorn-themed products have been super popular over the last few years, and I think our blend works with well with anything 'unicorn'- inspired; it is really pretty and super sparkly.

If you could improve one thing about how your run your business, what would it be?

Definitely seeking more help when needed. I recently started working with a local photographer and a graphic designer which gives me more time to focus on the other aspects of Sparkle Town.

I am also planning to take on additional team members, so watch this space!

What are you most proud of in your business?

I am really proud that I built my business completely from scratch.

I also get to spend every day doing something that has a positive impact and that also gives me the flexibility to spend time with my children.

Quickfire questions

Where do you live?

I live in Hertfordshire with my husband Alex and our two children. We moved here seven years ago from North London, and it was definitely the right decision for us! We are surrounded by so much greenery and have the countryside right on our doorstep.

Do you have a favourite Sparkle Town product?

That is a tricky one! Can I choose all of them? It usually depends on my mood: one day I might be feeling particularly pink, another day I find that one of the glitter mixes suits me best!

Do you have any hobbies?

I love curling up with a good book (if I have the time, that is).

I also consider myself an enthusiastic – but highly unskilled – gardener!

Creatively, I love candle making and would like to learn pottery, resin art and soap making. If only there were more hours in the day...

I also love to travel. I spent much of my twenties working and travelling in other countries and hope to show my children more of this beautiful planet.

Favourite place to be?

I love the Greek Islands so a beautiful Greek beach would be at the very top of my list to visit.

You can visit Josie's website at

www.sparkletown.co.uk

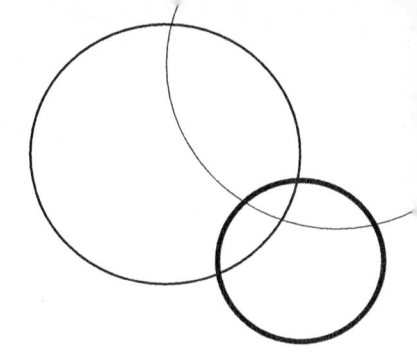

Before you go...

You may have chosen this book because you wanted to try a new craft, or make products you would normally buy in the shops, for a fraction of the price. You may have also chosen this book because you have an idea that you think you would be good at and make money from.

Whatever your reasons, I hope you have had fun! Who knew that making wax melts would connect you with hundreds of other like-minded people and empty your bank account whenever new fragrance oils and glitters were released?

When I was interviewing wax-melt makers and suppliers for the book, I noticed that we all shared the same views about this particular craft, namely:

- Learning to make wax melts can be easy and fairly cheap (if you have a starter kit, for example, or this book - yay), but if you want to experiment further and/or sell quality products, serious investment of both money and time is required to succeed

- Try not to lose heart if you do not get much customer interest at first; focus on what makes you stand out and change what doesn't (sounds simple, right?)

- There is no 'right' or 'wrong' wax to use. Choose whatever wax works for you

- It can get very addictive, very quickly

- It is vital to believe in yourself!

Making and selling wax melts is definitely a journey and I hope this book has made yours an enjoyable and simpler one.

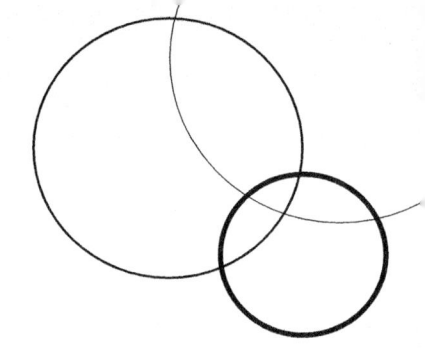

Acknowledgments

I would like to thank all the wax melt makers featured in this book: Alice Naylor of Melt Me Real Good, Fiona Nottingham of Ofina and Danielle Small of The Hertford Candle Co. Thank you for sharing your advice and experiences in this book; I look forward to seeing the next steps you take with your businesses.

Thank you to Louise Clark of Oasis Oils and Josie Boulter of Sparkle Town for your interviews. It was a pleasure to chat with you both and a privilege to be let into your worlds.

Thank you to those who helped bring the book to life: Hazel for editing, Ken for the designs and Kate for typesetting. I am incredibly fortunate to have worked with such patient and skilled professionals!

Finally, a huge thank you to my husband for everything he does for me.

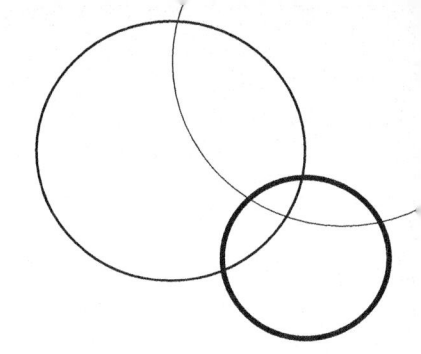

About the author

Zoe George has been making and selling candles, wax melts and other home fragrance products for several years. She shares her knowledge and enthusiasm for these handmade crafts in a series called The Home Fragrance Workbooks.

Zoe lives in London with her husband and has a super-friendly Labrador named Max.

Printed in Great Britain
by Amazon